It's About Time

It's About Time

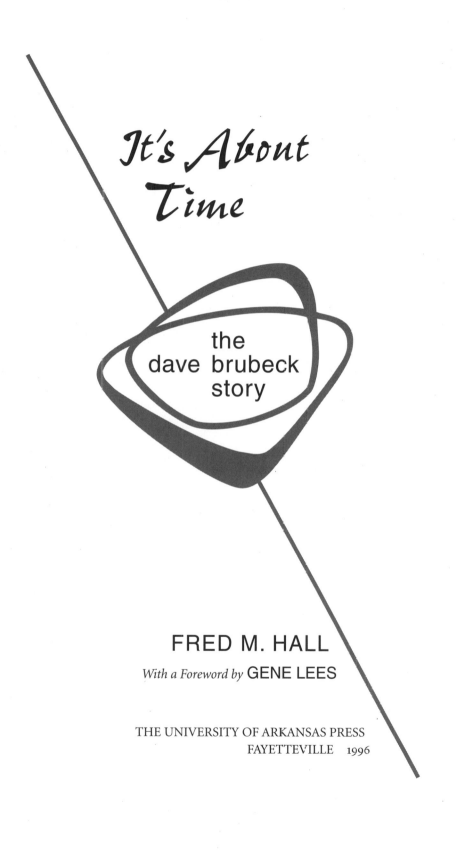

the
dave brubeck
story

FRED M. HALL

With a Foreword by GENE LEES

THE UNIVERSITY OF ARKANSAS PRESS
FAYETTEVILLE   1996

00   99   98   97   96   5   4   3   2

Designed by Gail Carter

⊛ The paper used in this publication meets the minimum
requirements of the American National Standard for
Permanence of Paper for Printed Library Materials Z39.48-1984.

Library of Congress Cataloging-in-Publication Data
Hall, Fred, 1923–
It's about time : the Dave Brubeck story / Fred M. Hall.
p.   cm.
ISBN 1-55728-404-0 (cloth : alk. paper). — ISBN 1-55728-405-0 (pbk. : alk. paper)
1. Brubeck, Dave.   2. Jazz musicians — United States — Biography.
I. Title.
ML410.B868H35   1996
781.65'092—dc20
[B]   95-38531
                                                   CIP
                                                   MN

Lyrics to "Strange Meadowlark," written by Iola Brubeck, copyright © 1963,
renewed 1991 by Derry Music Company, are reprinted by permission.

Poem "Once When I Was Very Young" by Michael Brubeck,
edited by John Jenney (also published as a song with music by Dave Brubeck),
copyright © 1987 by Derry Music Company, reprinted here by permission.

Untitled poem by Michael Brubeck, copyright © 1995
by Michael L. Brubeck, is reprinted here by permission of author.

Quotes from the "Dave Brubeck Quartet Newsletter" and from liner notes
by Dave Brubeck used by permission of Dave and Iola Brubeck.

Every effort has been made where previously published material
is quoted to obtain permission for use here.

For Gita

Acknowledgments

This book was conceived both as a history of the life and times of David Warren Brubeck and as a study of those who were part of the Classic Brubeck Quartet, easily the most successful and possibly still the most popular of the long-lived jazz groups. Paul Desmond, Eugene "Senator" Wright, and Joe Morello play a central part. But Dave, and thus jazz history, was shaped by his family, the cowboys on the ranch that was his home throughout his teenage years, the many musicians with whom he worked and studied, his GI buddies in Europe during World War II, and the music-industry figures who guided his recording career. Most of all, Dave's career decisions were driven by his family: six children and his wife, Iola, whose encouragement and innovative (and protective) judgment made possible the commercial and artistic achievements that are virtually unparalleled in a field where just making a living is a hard-won success.

Happily for me, cooperation was warmly supplied by Dave and Iola and resulted in more than a hundred in-person and telephone interviews with them, including long sessions at their home in Connecticut and on the road before and after concerts. I cannot thank them enough for their time and effort in researching places, events, times, and people. They also supplied countless photographs and leads for supplemental interviews.

Chris, Dan, Matthew, and Michael, the Brubeck sons, also gave generously of their time, as did their sister, Catherine Brubeck Yaghsizian. The same must be said of the extended Brubeck family. Among these I especially thank George Moore, Russell Gloyd, Richard Jeweler, Frank Modica, and Juliet Gerlin.

A number of Dave's key musical associates consented to be interviewed at length to provide the kind of anecdotal material that only they possessed. Most important were drummer Joe Morello and bassist Gene Wright. Morello I found at his drum school in New Jersey. Wright invited me into his home and studio not once, but several times. His bookshelves are filled with the most comprehensive collection of memorabilia of the Quartet's travels and triumphs to be found anywhere.

Among other musical associates, I spoke with clarinetist Bill Smith at Dave and Iola's fiftieth anniversary party in 1992. He and Dave have made music together since their Mills College days immediately after the war. Randy Jones, Jack Six, and Gerry Mulligan reminisced freely about Brubeck and his music. Cumulatively, their observations illustrate why and how making music with Dave has always been such a special joy.

Friends from boyhood days and college times with whom I spoke included Bob Skinner, Newell Johnson, and Jack Toomay.

To learn more about the war years and Dave's part in the European campaigns, I called upon that one-of-a-kind chronicler of twentieth-century American history, Studs Terkel. He, in turn, sent me to Leroy Pearlman (aka Ray Wax), who, as you will see, probably saved Dave's life on the eve of his first battle as a lowly rifleman with Patton's army.

The times immediately after the "Good War" and into the 1950s were illuminated by conversations with Howard Brubeck, Dave's brother; Jimmy and Laurel Lyons; Carl Jefferson; Peter Levinson; Johnny Mathis; Grover Sales; and the co-owners of the legendary Blackhawk jazz club in San Francisco, Guido Cacianti and John and Helen Noga. Brubeck discoverer and Columbia Records producer George Avakian talked with me in his home just up the Hudson from New York City.

Among the critics interviewed were Leonard Feather and Doug Ramsey. Ramsey and Gene Lees were especially valuable in helping me to understand the elusive, somewhat mysterious Paul Desmond. Marian McPartland helped greatly in assessing Dave Brubeck the piano player.

Once the actual writing began, help came from a number of sources. I'd especially like to express my gratitude to that prolific writer Jim McKimmey for his early support in many ways, including his research of Dave's 1941 summer at Lake Tahoe.

Editor-writer Marvin Sosna contributed much time and talent. Marvin's credentials as a long-time reviewer and critic of both classical and jazz music inform the chapter on Brubeck's "serious" music and other sections of the book as well.

I'm indebted to veteran editor Jonathan Leff for his invariably correct suggestions on style and my fine editor at the University of Arkansas Press, Brian King, for his excellent advice and faithfulness to my text and intent.

My partner in the final months of writing was my stepson, Michael Lewis. His training and experience in journalism, music, and computer arts made possible much of the editing, the polishing, and the coping with today's technical requirements in publishing. There's no way to thank him sufficiently.

As to printed references, I especially relied on Ted Gioia's definitive study of West Coast Jazz, Doug Ramsey's copious liner notes for the Columbia Dave Brubeck box-set, Leonard Feather's *Encyclopedia of Jazz*, and Gene Lees' *Jazzletter*.

Finally, the chores of editing and writing were made easier and surer by the contributions of my wife, Gita, who accompanied me on all the travels required for the preparation of this book. Her wise influence benefits all herein. She, in fact, suggested (insisted) that I take on this project and helped me follow through as she has done for more than forty-three exciting and loving years.

Contents

Foreword

It would seem a contradiction in terms to say that one of the most successful jazz musicians in history is underrated, but I suggest that in Dave Brubeck's case this may well be so. The explanation lies in a tendency in the "jazz community" to distrust success. An unexamined premise is that because so much that is immensely successful in our culture is meretricious, *anything* that is successful is by definition bad. The first inversion of that chord is that what is obscure and admired by few is automatically good.

This faith grows out of dubious reasoning, although that is perhaps an inappropriate term, since there is little reasoning at all involved. It is, to use a term coined probably by the late Leonard Feather, the hipper-than-thou attitude. And although it reaches great heights in the jazz community, it is not confined to jazz. Witness the years of condescension toward Tchaikovsky and Grieg, generated by the fact that audiences genuinely liked their music. And the inversion of *that* chord is that only music that must be supported by grants from foundations because the public is indifferent to it is really good. The smaller the audience, this attitude holds, the better the music must be. Mozart's music was long considered to be light and saccharine. Time has led to an altered evaluation. Probably the most popular composers in concert music are Bach, Beethoven, and Mozart—not bad writers.

There is no correlation between popularity, or lack of it, and merit.

Time is bringing a reevaluation of the career of Dave Brubeck and the quartet that for so many years included the superb saxophonist Paul Desmond. Paul hasn't been given his due lately, either: he was one of the most astonishingly inventive and melodic improvisers jazz has ever known, and the most lyrical. Dave is being seen in his full value as a composer and, more and more, as a pianist.

A biography was overdue. And Fred Hall undertook the task of creating one.

As this book neared completion, Fred had been in radio broadcasting for fifty-four years. He started in 1941, when he was a seventeen-year-old engineer with a Washington, D.C., radio station and then the Mutual Broadcasting System, doing dance-band radio remotes. He did broadcasts of bands from such places as the Hotel Lincoln in New York, the Steel Pier in Atlantic City, and the Glen Island Casino on Long Island. It was during this time that he met all the major band leaders and made friends with many of them, some of whom remained friends for life.

He also accumulated an encyclopedic knowledge of broadcasting. There are few persons who understand as Fred does the symbiotic relationship between network broadcasting and popular music at that time, for the big-band era was founded on and sustained by network broadcasting. If it was a golden age of song—and it was because of the music of Arlen, Porter, Gershwin, Kern, Rogers, Youmans, Carmichael, Warren—it came to pass because network radio supported it and the bands played it. The withdrawal of the major broadcasting companies from network radio in favor of television was one of the factors that ended the age of great songs and the concomitant age of big bands, both of which were inextricably linked in destiny.

Fred's knowledge of the band era is phenomenal. After he interviewed Paul Weston and his wife, Jo Stafford, Jo said that he knew more about their careers than they did.

I met Fred one Sunday morning when I was visiting Ojai, California, for the weekend. A clock radio in the motel went on automatically, and I heard first Count Basie, then Jack Jones, and a man who discussed them with great knowledge. This brought me to full wakefulness, and when I heard the station's call letters, I telephoned and spoke to him. That's how I met Fred. He invited me to visit the station, which I did later that morning. It was in part because of this encounter that I moved to Ojai and came to know Fred very well.

Fred spent World War II in the navy, with much of his duty time with the Armed Forces Radio Service in the South Pacific (Dave Brubeck was slogging across Europe as an infantryman). After the war Fred went back into radio in both engineering and programming and became a network newsman and feature writer-producer for Mutual Radio and ABC Radio. All the while he honed his ability as an interviewer, with guests that included countless band leaders, sidemen, singers, arrangers, and composers. Then Fred built, owned, and sold a string of radio stations, prompting me to call him a Johnny Appleseed of broadcasting. In recent years he has produced and hosted a show called *Swing Thing,* which is syndicated to stations all over the United States, Canada, and the British Isles. He wrote two books that incorporated many of his music-related interviews, called *Dialogues in Swing* and *More Dialogues in Swing.* He does this from his home studio in Lake Tahoe, California—he moved there several years ago. His collection of twenty-seven thousand records, CDs, and tapes weighs three tons. The tapes of his twenty-six hundred hours of broadcasts, many of them incorporating interviews with the artists, constitute one of the great audio documentations of American popular music and jazz ever accumulated, perhaps exceeded only by the taped broadcasts of Willis Conover for the Voice of America.

Fred had interviewed Dave Brubeck several times. He wanted to do a biography of Dave. It became a passion, a story that he as a former newsman realized was being missed. He discussed it with Dave and Dave's wife, Iola, and the work began. Fred brought to bear his reserves of knowledge of music and of the age he and Dave had both lived through.

Fred's sympathetic study of a great musician is the result. History will thank him for it.

GENE LEES

It's About Time

Time to Begin

He was a lanky, skinny, bright-eyed sixteen-year-old. He was a cowboy in the true sense of that word. But in 1936, David Warren Brubeck had a recurrent and very uncowboylike dream: "There was this ballroom, about twelve miles from the end of our ranch. My dream in those days was that the Benny Goodman band would be coming through on their band bus and I wouldn't let 'em through the cattle. I had herded hundreds of cattle on the road. Then, I'd get on the bus and naturally, like a *B* movie, there'd be a piano right on the bus, and I'd be discovered! I had that dream for hours a day."

Dave Brubeck was born in Concord, California, on December 6, 1920. At that time Concord, about thirty miles east and slightly north of San Francisco, was a town of about twenty-six hundred persons, typical of the small communities that dotted most of the United States. In the next half-century it would absorb its share of the Bay Area's urban sprawl, becoming a congested residential and business center and the home of Carl Jefferson's Concord Jazz Records. When the city of Concord staged its first jazz festival, there were more than three times as many people in the audience to hear

Dave play as there had been in Concord's entire population during Dave's youth. Dave, who remembers his roots, says, "The [Concord] Pavilion is situated on land that was once a ranch my dad rented. His cattle grazed where the pavilion is now. I knew Carl Jefferson before he had anything to do with jazz. He was a Lincoln-Mercury dealer, probably the biggest in California."

Dave was the youngest of three sons born to Howard "Pete" and Elizabeth Ivey "Bessie" Brubeck. The Brubeck name, says Dave, is "either German or Scottish. It means 'by the brook' in Scottish. My mother was Polish and/or Russian—she used to say 'White Russian'; she wasn't sure—and English." Dave's father was born in the town of Amedee, on Honey Lake, in the mostly desert county of Lassen in California's far-northeastern corner. This is starkly beautiful country that blooms with wildflowers of every color after the winter snows and rains. The sky is endless and the horizon clear.

Dave's grandfather, Lewis Warren Brubeck, ran two hotels in Amedee. Lewis grew up in Albany, Indiana, but when he was twenty-one, his father gave him a horse, and he came west to California to homestead, taking advantage of the Desert Land Act of Lassen County of 1875. In 1877, he married Louisa Grass. That union resulted in eight children, Howard Peter among them. One of the children, a daughter, died in childhood.

In 1890, a narrow-gauge railroad, the Nevada-California-Oregon, completed tracks that began in Reno, Nevada, and terminated on the east side of Honey Lake. The new terminus was soon named Amedee in honor of Amedee Deoau Moran, one of the owners of the N-C-O. Lewis Brubeck had previously purchased 151 acres at the site on Honey Lake where he had lived since the massacre by Indians of the Pearson family there in 1868. He foresaw a prosperous future for Amedee and built a two-story hotel, complete with two dining rooms, eight guest rooms, a big kitchen, a ladies' parlor, and, of course, a spacious bar. He named the place the Pioneer Hotel. Two years later he bought the Amedee Hotel, which had been built just across the tracks. He ran both hotels, along with bathhouses (plentiful natural hot springs dot the area) and the post office.

Dave says, "From Amedee north, anything had to go by horse or mule. Teams of twenty mules or horses would be driven there from Oregon to pick up what was shipped across the country by railroad—furniture, household goods, things like that. From Amedee it would be taken on what was the Oregon Trail to Portland and other northwestern places. The hotel housed all the teamsters. They could stay all night in dormitory-like facilities and eat three meals for fifty cents."

Amedee did indeed become a boom town in 1892, and until he bought the rival hotel across the tracks, Lewis had to use his livery stable to house the overflow. More than two hundred people were fed daily in the dining room.

All went well, as national publicity about the hot springs brought tourists and settlers to Amedee. But trouble came for Lewis when Miss Maud Bentle, who worked at the Amedee Hotel as a telegrapher, committed suicide. Lewis was charged with keeping an inn in a disorderly manner, found guilty of a misdemeanor, and fined two hundred dollars. That was in 1894. Four years later there was a murder at the hotel. Lewis apparently began to wonder if it was all worth it. He bought a seventeen-hundred-acre cattle ranch down in Contra Costa County and sold all his Amedee holdings in late 1900. All surviving children made the move south, thus setting the scene for Pete to meet Bessie and found a musical dynasty.

Amedee itself quickly declined, and when the Southern Pacific Railroad took over the N-C-O and moved the tracks east of Amedee in 1922, the die was cast for the community to become a ghost town. The post office closed in 1924 and, in 1950, in a delinquent tax sale, Jack and Margaret Humphrey became sole owners of what was left of Amedee, which is now used as part of their ranching operations. They paid a total of $32.15 for 643 town lots.

The bloodlines of German, Polish, Russian, and English are easy to establish. But what about American Indian? The first thing that will hit you, seeing Dave or any of his sons close-up, is the striking element of Native American in the strong, angular, hawklike features. If you ask Dave if he is part Indian, he is likely to say, "Maybe." But so dominant are the physical characteristics that many of his friends and associates have simply taken it for granted that those genes were strong ones. There was evidently considerable controversy about this among elder family members, but Dave's nickname from his teenage years has been "Geronimo" and later "Cochise." Some said that Dave's grandfather had been married three times and that one of his wives may have been an Indian woman. This could make Dave one-fourth Northern Paiute, which was the tribe that lived in the area of Pyramid Lake.

By the time Dave was twelve and growing up on a ranch near Ione, California, he knew many Miwoks, an Indian group recently re-granted tribal status. There was a small Indian *rancheria* (with a sweat house) on the ranch. One of Dave's closest friends, Al Walloupe, was a full Miwok and Pete's top cowhand.

The marriage of Pete and Bessie was not the joining of kindred souls. Dave calls it, "Impossible. No one could figure it out." Bessie was cultured, intensely musical, sophisticated in her interests. Pete was a rough-and-tough cowboy: a perfect example of the great American westerner. Dave's brother Howard said shortly before his death in February 1993, "I think they had an enormous physical attraction for each other, and I think both of them had this ability to respect what the other was."

Bessie was the daughter of a livery stable owner in Concord. He drove the stagecoach over the hills to Oakland to where the Claremont Hotel stands today. The property on which the hotel stands and more than a thousand acres around it were once held by Lewis Brubeck's family. Dave says, "My mother's father needed horses for his livery stable—he was like Hertz rent-a-horse. Pete Brubeck came into Concord with two cattle cars—one of horses, one of cattle—to sell. He was maybe fourteen, maybe sixteen at the time. My mother's father was at the corral when my dad arrived, and they immediately liked each other. So that night, when Mom's dad came home for supper, he said, 'I met a *real* young man at the corrals today.' He invited the young man home for dinner soon after that because he was so impressed with somebody who had all this responsibility so young. That's how my mom and dad met and fell in love."

In Concord, Bessie was able to get to nearby San Francisco (by electric train and ferry) for the symphony and other cultural events. She longed to be a concert pianist and had studied with the best teachers in the area. In 1926, when Dave was in first grade, she went to England to study with Tobias Matthay and Dame Myra Hess, taking along Dave's older brother Henry for companionship. Bessie also worked over many years to earn a college degree, going part time or summers to San Jose State, the University of California at Berkeley, and the University of Idaho. But when Dave was twelve, Pete was hired as a ranch manager for the H. Moffat family's forty-five-thousand-acre Rancho Arroyo Seco near Ione, about forty miles northeast of Stockton, which was devoted almost entirely to cattle.

Ione was then a small rural center; it is still, in 1995, a town with a prairie feel, its horizon broad, a few shade trees gracefully arching over sparsely-populated streets. Bessie, now cut off from reasonably easy access to cultural events, continued to teach piano and coached a talented Indian girl, Ramona Burris, as an assistant. Bessie had brought three pianos with her from Concord: an upright, on which she taught her students, and two grand pianos for recitals in her studio. The studio was in the home the Brubecks rented in Ione itself—the ranch house serving primarily as headquarters for the cowboys.

Rancho Arroyo Seco was no gentleman's weekend toy. It had originally been a Spanish land grant. The original boundaries of the ranch ran from the Stockton-to-Sacramento road to the foothills of the Sierras, from the Cosumnes River to the Mokelumne River. The present ranch consists mostly of rolling, semi-arid country really only suitable for cattle grazing. The original ranch house had been built as a garrison for a Mexican cavalry unit. According to Dave, the pantry where he used to separate the cream from the milk had adobe walls three feet thick to protect against marauders. In 1993 the house was still standing and occupied; the property, now reduced to a mere thirty-two thousand acres and having changed hands several times, belonged again to part of the Moffat family.

Dave's father was more than a rancher and cattle buyer. He was one of the top ropers in the state. He won, among many other such events, the steer roping, double-team steer roping, and calf roping at the Salinas Rodeo. In those days, Salinas was the country's top rodeo event. Of course Pete Brubeck wanted Dave to become a cowboy and take up the ranching life, and that was Dave's original intention as well. But Dave's mother fought constantly to protect Dave's hands, and he was forbidden to practice some dangerous roping techniques.

Bessie Brubeck had managed to guide both older boys into music. The eldest son, Henry, became a violinist and a drummer. As a professional musician, he played drums primarily. The violin was, however, his favorite instrument. He was with Del Courtney's Orchestra, one of the best of the so-called "hotel" bands, and then he became the first drummer with Gil Evans, who became one of the postbop icons in the 1950s. Henry started his long teaching career in Lompoc, California, and later moved to Santa Barbara, where he was superintendent of music in the public schools and head of the high-school music department. His marching bands won many awards and played in the Rose Bowl, and his student orchestra was considered one of the nation's best high-school performing groups.

Howard Brubeck, the middle son, had a long and distinguished career as composer and educator, retiring as dean of humanities at Palomar College in California. Throughout the years, he was a guiding light and sometime teacher to Dave. After the success began for the Brubeck Quartet, it was Howard who usually did the transcribing of performances for print music and instruction books. As a composer, Howard is most noted for *Dialogues for Jazz Combo and Orchestra*, which Dave and the Quartet recorded with the New York Philharmonic under Leonard Bernstein in 1959.

Dave studied piano under his mother's tutelage. She found him to be anything but a conventional student. He says, "I wouldn't conform to the very basic piano instruction. I didn't play classical music. I couldn't read, but boy, could I fake reading! I knew all the keyboard exercises, hearing my mother's other students practice them. Finally my mother caught on and gave up on me. So, at eleven, I didn't have to practice anymore."

Dave's reading difficulty probably stemmed from the fact he was born cross-eyed. He wore glasses in the cradle. Those heavy, tortoise-rim, bebop glasses became a trademark when the Quartet hit it big, but he somehow outgrew the vision problem in late middle age. Dave never became a prolific music reader, although he could later write music and compose major vocal works as well as complex scores for small and large groups of instruments. He composed his first music when he was four, which his mother wrote down for him.

He was on horseback after school and all summer long from age twelve until he went away to college. Dave says it could get hot on the range. "When your tongue is sticking out a mile and you're driving cattle, you can see the snow-peaked mountains in the distance. That adds an insult to how thirsty you are." Year-round, Dave had to milk the cow, morning and evening. He had to carry all the wood—a big job, since the cookstove for the ranch hands was going from four in the morning until after dinner at night. In the summer, he had to carry all the drinking water uphill to the house because the well was in the meadow below.

Dave says, "That made me pretty strong, those two jobs." He also learned discipline because as much as getting the job done was important, it had to be done on time. "If I goofed, my dad would get me out of bed in the middle of the night. That woodpile had to be full or I was in trouble."

"Still," Dave says, "I think my mind was always on music, whether I was riding a horse, or what."

Dave was paid a dollar a day for his ranch work in the summer, most of which he saved. Earlier, in Concord, he sold apples and had a newspaper route, getting up early each morning to go to the railroad station where they'd throw the papers off the train, and he would deliver them all over town. A precedent was established: hard work and long hours. These became invaluable traits when the time came for Dave to support a family as a working musician. So was his habit of saving every possible penny. His insistence on never missing an engagement also stemmed from his childhood. As many as sixty years later in the fall of 1992 during a European tour, seventy-two-year-old Dave Brubeck refused to stop concertizing even though twice he had to be rushed to the hospital to be given emergency cardiac assistance, probably brought on by the severe flu he had suffered from for weeks. That incident was an example of his belief that once you take on the job, you have to do it. A few years before, Dave had insisted on resuming concerts just six weeks after open-heart surgery for a multiple bypass. Dave didn't grow up to be a cowboy, but his father's work ethic was tightly instilled in him. So was his total devotion to family.

Dave was very close to his father. A lifelong friend and Concord neighbor was Bob Skinner, who also became an accomplished pianist. They lived next door to each other, and Bob Skinner was one of the first persons invited to Dave and Iola's fiftieth wedding anniversary celebration in 1992. Skinner recalls that he and Dave would often be taken by Pete Brubeck on long camping trips in the Sierras and that Pete taught his son much of what he knew about ranching. There was no doubt he was hoping Dave would be the son to follow him in the saddle. But this was not to happen. Middle son Howard (four and a half years older than Dave) pointed out that, "He wanted us to be whatever we wanted to be. He didn't give a damn what that was. And he was enough of a man himself and had confidence enough in himself as a man that he didn't need his sons to prove him. He just supported us in every possible way he could. He was a gift from God. My dad was something else, especially for a guy with a second-grade education."

By his midteens, Dave was playing casuals, occasional one-time musical engagements in local venues, but he still thought of himself as a cowboy and lived that life to the fullest. "I used to go with my dad to places like Fallon, Nevada [near Reno], when he was on the road buying cattle or helping at other ranches. The H. Moffat Company had ranches in Elko, Nevada, and throughout the area. You have to feed the cattle in the winter, and there'd be six feet of snow out there, sometimes. Cattle dying, no helicopters to drop hay. It was a tough life. But then, my dad being Number One Roper made you feel pretty good." It's clear that Dave thought of his father as a heroic figure.

While Dave never questioned that his future lay in ranching or something closely related, he lived with music. Polyrhythms countered the gait of his horse while herding cattle. Indian and Spanish rhythms and melodies were still heard in a part of California where Spanish land grants and a dwindling population of Native Americans had a century before given way to seekers of gold. Music was a constant at home, with piano recitals and chamber music and choir practice. Mostly classics or light classics were played on the wind-up phonograph when Dave was young: Sousa marches, some opera, and, rarely, lighter fare like "The Two Black Crows." At age eight or nine, Dave would go next door to Bob Skinner's house to play records that interested him more—"mostly Teddy Wilson."

Later, in Ione, the family had both a more modern phonograph and a radio on which Dave began to hear big bands and jazz. A particular favorite was the Billy Kyle Trio. Kyle was also the pianist with John Kirby's Biggest Little Band, which had a weekly show on NBC that attracted Dave as a regular listening ritual. The broadcasts featured Kirby's wife of that time, Maxine Sullivan.

All America had become radio crazy by the mid-1930s, and Dave, who could hear the powerhouse key network stations in San Francisco, was certainly no exception despite school work and the never-ending chores on the ranch. Since Benny Goodman's first *Let's Dance* coast-to-coast broadcasts in late 1934 (succeeded later by *The Camel Caravan*), the young cowboy had listened avidly to the big bands. Still, it was the small jazz groups he enjoyed the most.

The first record Dave bought with the savings he had worked long and hard for was Fats Waller's "There's Honey on the Moon Tonight," backed by "Let's Be Fair and Square in Love." The young cowboy admired the playing of Teddy Wilson with the Benny Goodman Trio and Quartet. He liked Albert Ammons and Meade Lux Lewis, the great boogie-woogie pioneers. Dave heard and was suitably astounded by Art Tatum. Just how much these jazz greats influenced his later playing is arguable. In Dave's easy-swing, locked-hands performances, however, there were traces of Billy Kyle, pianist with John Kirby and later Louis Armstrong, and Milt Buckner, famed for his work with Lionel Hampton. He was crazy about the playing of both Count Basie and Duke Ellington. Ellington later became a good and valuable friend, supporter, and admirer. To many listeners, Dave's tribute to Ellington, "The Duke," captures the essence of the romantic, chromatic, and witty Ellington persona. It has proved to be one of Brubeck's most played and recorded compositions.

At fourteen or fifteen, Dave had begun to gig around, mostly on weekends. The Swing Era was about to dominate young America; but among most White orchestras, whether national, regional, or local, the jazz influence was at best tentative. Ballads were done straight, and novelties were done "cute." Big-band jazz was most likely to manifest itself as a "Casa Loma Stomp" killer-diller. Fletcher Henderson's Benny Goodman arrangements were yet to become the departure point for bands and dancers alike.

Ione itself offered little or no opportunity. Known in the gold-rush days as "Bedbug," it was a community of less than a thousand and had grown only marginally sixty years later. But Dave found piano gigs with a band in Jackson and Angels Camp and at an outdoor dance hall near Clements on the Mokelumne River. This ranch-raised teenager who could not read music played alongside professional musicians for paying audiences. The band was led by, as Dave remembers, "the man who picked up our laundry at the ranch. He heard me playing when he came to the house one day, and he asked me if I wanted to play with him. His name was Johnny Ostabah, from Lodi, the town just below Sacramento. He had a band job Saturday nights at the Clements Dance Hall on the river." It was a time when people all over America wanted to dance and wanted live music to dance to. Dance halls in towns across the nation filled with couples on weekends.

In his senior year in high school, Dave recalls, "I played with Bill Amick at Sutter Creek, Jackson, Placerville, and Angels Camp—places like that. We played stock arrangements of popular tunes of the day."

How did Dave handle the problem of not being able to read music? "I faked it good enough so they didn't know, and I didn't tell them." Dave says they played tunes like "Please Be Kind," written in 1938 by Sammy Cahn and his first collaborator, Saul Chaplin, for a one-reel movie comedy. Brubeck always loved that tune and included it in his 1992 MusicMaster collection, *Once When I Was Very Young*. Then there was "Boo Hoo," "Heigh Ho," "Once in a While," "Harbor Lights"—tunes that have become associated in memory with Guy Lombardo and Sammy Kaye—and "I'm an Old Cow-Hand," not the kind of material that you might predict as antecedent to Dave's later propensity for 5/4 time. About as close to jazz as the band got was a sort of quasi Dixieland, with Dave faking such chestnuts as "Tiger Rag" and "Twelfth Street Rag." Hard to imagine Dave Brubeck playing honky-tonk, but it was one of the styles of that day.

In his first year in college, Dave returned on weekends to pick up a dollar or two with the Amick guys. Hundreds of these little "territory" bands managed to stay alive in the dance-crazy America of the thirties. That provided good experience for any young player: a chance for seasoning, the building of self-confidence, and learning of all the wonderful songs that later became solid standards (as well as some terrible passing-pops).

As Dave passed his junior year in high school, his mother became more and more insistent that he go to college. If Dave went to college, it became clear it would be to College of the Pacific (COP) in Stockton, where brother Henry had been a student, a fraternity leader, editor of the college yearbook, and a drummer in the Del Courtney band. Howard enrolled in COP but left after a few weeks to attend San Francisco State, where he says there existed the best music department in California for training teachers of music.

Remember that Dave was the only son to actually live on Arroyo Seco Ranch. Henry, by then, was playing drums with Del Courtney and Gil Evans in Stockton. Howard had stayed behind in Concord to teach and to play organ at the Presbyterian church, living in the same family home into which his mother and her parents had moved when his mother was only a few months old. It was the house in which all three Brubeck sons had been born.

Pete Brubeck certainly encouraged his youngest son to continue the family tradition of ranching. However, Bessie wanted Dave to be exposed to a wider world. When Dave graduated from grammar school, Pete gave him four Holstein cows worth, in those days, about twenty dollars each. Pete kept careful records of their descendants as the herd grew. They remained Dave's even after it became certain his career would be in music.

In 1937, however, a future in music was far from being clearly defined and thus, when the youngest son finally agreed to leave the ranch to go to college, it was to be as a premedical veterinary student. "It was a compromise," says Dave. "I'd become a veterinarian and come right back to ranch and join my dad!" Had that happened, Dave Brubeck might never have met Iola Whitlock and there'd be no Brubeck family of Darius, Michael, Catherine, Chris, Daniel, and Matthew. There would have been no international fame for the Dave Brubeck Quartet, and the world would not have been enriched by that great body of Brubeck music, on paper, live, and recorded, that eventually reached to the farthest of faraway places.

Time to Learn

Inorganic chemistry, zoology, algebra, and microbiology proved to be less than fascinating to the youngest Brubeck son, who was a working cowboy whose knowledge of animals, to this point, had been largely practical. Dave didn't embrace the academic life, and to be fair, academia was a little dubious of Dave Brubeck.

Stockton, California, is an inland seaport serving the fertile San Joaquin Valley with a seventy-seven-mile channel direct to San Francisco Bay. In the first third of the twentieth century, it was best known for its canneries, food-packing houses, paper products, walnuts, and, as time went by, for pleasure boating. In the later 1930s it was a smallish, rough-and-ready city in which the College of the Pacific, at the then-outskirts of town, was a cultural oasis. Stockton had lured COP to relocate from San Jose, using an offer of free land contributed by the city as an inducement. These days, COP is University of the Pacific, a full, four-year college with graduate programs. When Dave attended, it was actually two schools on the same campus: a state-funded two-year college called Stockton Junior College and the Methodist, private College of the Pacific, sometimes referred to by students as "Senior College." This arrangement brought in money from the California State College system, income essential to the preservation of the private school during the depression years.

Dave, a freshman at age seventeen, lived first at Mrs. Anderson's boarding house, a place favored by the school for its moral fiber and by the parents of students for its low cost. It was just two blocks from the campus. All went well at first until one day he and a roommate, Red Johnson, got into a scuffle that had unfortunate repercussions.

This is the way Dave remembers the incident. "Red wanted to take a bath, but I had already drawn the water for *my* bath and got in the tub. Red came in and poured iodine, a whole bottle, in the water. I jumped out. We got into a scuffle, both of us naked, chasing each other around the boarding house, and kind of wrecked some doors, the floor, and some plumbing, causing floods all over the house. The dean removed us both from Mrs. Anderson's and forbade us from living any closer than one mile of the campus." This was atypical of Dave's behavior. Then, as now, he was more interested in making music than war of any sort.

Brubeck moved a mile away to Tuxedo Avenue, near the residence of Charles and Myrtle Whitlock and their daughter, Iola, whom he had not yet met. He just had a room, no board. Dave remembers eating corn flakes and canned peaches for breakfast every day. Neither required refrigeration or heating. He came to despise both, an enduring antipathy. He remembers filling his stomach at one big meal each day, generally at a Chinese restaurant. Dave recalls he had seven-course meals for thirty-five cents.

A second move found him living in the back of a garage in an unfinished room with a cement floor. By then he had, however, acquired a piano—a beat-up Starr upright that had (barely) survived the 1906 San Francisco earthquake. Apparently the instrument had been evacuated from a threatened house during the awful fire that followed the initial quake and was left sitting on the street during some backfiring. Dave says the shellac was all bubbly on one side. It played just fine, however, and was the source of endless pleasure for both Brubeck and his musician buddies. Dave had an active social life at school, although he returned home every weekend to play with the Bill Amick band, which helped to keep his fingers in shape and to support his schooling. He had numerous girlfriends, and there were guys like Ernie Farmer, John Dennis, and trumpet-player Newell Johnson, with whom he formed friendships that have lasted a lifetime. All three attended his half-century wedding anniversary party in 1992.

The final housing change in his senior year landed Dave and his friends in a basement flat they called the "Bomb Shelter." The Starr piano was there, along with a cookstove and a cold-water faucet. Harold Meeske (also at the anniversary celebration fifty years later) was Dave's sole roommate until one day, unannounced and unexpected, saxophonist Dave Van Kriedt moved in. "He was working with my old friend Bob Skinner in Oakland, and I'd gone down to hear Bob and wound up sitting in," Dave remembers. "Next thing I knew, Van Kriedt was at [the College of the] Pacific. He moved into the Bomb Shelter without saying a word. There was plenty of room—the whole basement of a house—and he went to all the classes he wanted to and never registered! One day he disappeared, without saying a word then, either, and he was gone." With or without Van Kriedt, there were constant jam sessions in that cellar. Often included was another tenor player, Darrell Cutler, who after the war became the leader of The Three D's, which was composed of Don Ratto, Darrell, and Dave. The three played and sang together in Stockton and San Francisco. Van Kriedt kept in touch, more or less, and, in fact, later introduced Dave to Paul Desmond. He was also to play an important part in the ground-breaking Octet of 1946.

There was an endless amount of great music to be heard in Stockton, Modesto, and Sacramento and even more in San Francisco and Oakland in 1940 and 1941. Thus Dave was able to hear many of the big bands in person, remembering especially Duke Ellington, Jimmy Lunceford, and, somewhat later, Stan Kenton. There were many small groups and solo artists like the now-legendary Cleo Brown, who indelibly impressed an all-ears Dave Brubeck. By the time Dave had moved to Senior College, he was gigging around with groups of various sizes in the Stockton area. But this activity began after it had become painfully apparent that he had no business being in the college's premed course of study in the first place.

In Dave's second year in Stockton, Dr. Arnold, the head of zoology, said, "Brubeck, your mind's not here. It's across the lawn in the conservatory. Please go there. Stop wasting my time and yours." Dave, needless to say, didn't fight this not-to-be-refused offer and transferred to the music department even though he still couldn't read music. A few years ago, he received a note backstage from this same professor. The note said, "Remember me? I'm the one who told you to move over to the conservatory."

In 1991 Dave told Gene Lees, in an interview for Gene's *Jazzletter*, "In order not to embarrass the family, I was pretty sure I could hide the fact that I couldn't read a note. Everything went well. You had to take a string instrument, a brass instrument, or a reed instrument. And when you're learning these instruments, it's all the scales and stuff that even somebody like myself could slip by the teacher." Dave was able to put off studying the keyboard until his senior year, faking his way through an increasingly adventurous interest in harmony and the ear training that had begun as a child. He became a favorite in class with Dr. J. Russell Bodley. During ear training, Bodley would say, "Can anyone listen to this progression and tell me what I've just played? Well, if nobody can, then wake up Brubeck." Dave told Lees, "In my own way, I could do it. He'd say, 'What chord is this?' and I'd say, 'That's the first chord in "Don't Worry 'bout Me."'" Then he'd say, 'Well, explain that, Mr. Brubeck.' I'd go play that chord. He'd say, 'Well, can't you say that's a flat ninth?' I didn't know it was a flat ninth. But that's the way I got through. Whatever I learned in harmony class I could apply that night playing in the club." But eventually, Dave had to take a keyboard instrument. "I thought, if I take organ, it'll be harder for them to know I can't read music yet. The first lesson, I left the damn electric organ on after my last practice. The teacher was furious. It was on all night, and he said, 'You could burn up an organ this way!' He kicked me out and gave me an F."

At this point a true crisis developed. The administration insisted that Dave take piano instruction. "I got a wonderful piano teacher, who figured out I couldn't read in about five minutes. She went to the dean and said, 'Brubeck can't read a note.'"

The dean called Dave in and told him he simply couldn't be graduated and, further, that Dave was a disgrace to the conservatory. Brubeck, whether defensively or defiantly, responded by saying, "It doesn't make any difference to me. I don't care whether I graduate or not. All I want to do is play jazz. I agree with you!"

But Dave had powerful supporters among the faculty. The counterpoint teacher, Horace I. Brown, told the dean that Brubeck composed the best counterpoint he'd ever seen in the class. And Dr. Bodley had similar praise and managed to convince the dean to let Dave graduate. There was one condition, however. Dave was "never to teach and embarrass the conservatory."

Dr. Bodley was Dave's number-one champion and supporter and the man who encouraged him the most at COP. Bodley was fully vindicated in his support forty-one years later when he drove from his home in Stockton to Sacramento to hear Dave's mass and a new work, the *Pange Lingua Variations,* commissioned by and premiered at the Cathedral of the Blessed Sacrament. The conservatory was never embarrassed. In fact, it finally awarded Dave Brubeck an honorary doctorate in music.

By his senior year, Dave was deeply involved in performing, with his playing ranging from accompanying the dance and gymnastics classes at COP for forty cents an hour to doing weekend gigs with the Tut Lombardo band in Modesto at the California Ballroom and the Wagon Wheel. Trumpeter Newell Johnson was also in that band. "It was a big band," he remembers, "and Dave didn't really like the idea of being the piano player in a large band because there was nothing for him to do but chord. We also played in small groups in some area nightclubs. They didn't pay anything, of course, maybe ten dollars a night. We did a lot of jamming, though, and for a while, Dave would sit in with Van Kriedt and others in San Francisco when he had free time. Then Dave organized his own big band. I was one of three trumpets. We had four saxes and three rhythm. We were very much in the Kenton style. We worked Memorial Auditorium in Stockton and Buddy Harpham did all the fantastic alto solos with Darrell Cutler on tenor. We played other locations, of course, including the summer of 1941 at Globin's in Tahoe."

Decades ago, within the limits of what is today the incorporated city of South Lake Tahoe, were individual townships with names such as Al Tahoe, Bijou, and Tahoe Valley. In 1924 Frank Globini arrived at Lake Tahoe from Marysville, California. A small, stocky, forceful man with a shrewd business sense and a gravel-throated voice, Globini purchased all of Al Tahoe as well as land that gave him access to the lake. Then he set up a business complex containing a hotel, which he named Globin's Al Tahoe, as well as a general store and service station.

The hotel was a large frame building crowned by an open-sided cupola atop a three-story section. The hotel included a dining room and a covered dance pavilion in the lake, reachable by a pier. It was to this hotel pier that high-school and college students summering at Lake Tahoe came to dance to bands from Sacramento, including that of Dick Jurgens.

And it was the new big band led by Dave Brubeck that Globini hired as his house band in the summer of 1941. Globini fired them the first night. This was a ploy that he used with all of his musicians. He would hire them, bring them in for one night, fire them, and then give them jobs around the hotel doing chores that earned rock-bottom pay. In effect, the music would be free.

Knowing that his brother Henry, in the Del Courtney band, had been similarly fired years before, Brubeck waited for Globini's next move, which was, "You wanna pick up nice piece of change, pump a little gas, see? That way I'll keep you on."

Not about to fall for it, Brubeck argued him out of the deal. Instead, an agreement was made that Brubeck and his musicians could obtain beds and sleep in a balcony over the dance floor on the lake. Wages were whatever came in at the door on Saturday night; food, however, had to be earned by playing in the dining area.

But the big band did not last long in Globin's dining room. The hotel owner appeared before the group early on and shouted with his gravelly voice, "Put sand in the horns!"

"What do you mean?" Brubeck asked, puzzled.

"Too loud!"

Brubeck softened the sound of his band, but the next night Globini reappeared and insisted, "Get rid of the horns!"

Brubeck complied. The big band played only on weekends. The dining-room music was diminished to a piano trio, which earned the food for the entire band—rice and green curried lamb, twice a day, for the rest of the summer.

Despite the monotonous and pungent quality of the sustenance, Brubeck found the experience richly rewarding. His bed, after all, was in a unique sort of naturally air-conditioned penthouse with a sweeping view of Lake Tahoe and its surrounding meadows and forest land. He was doing what he liked to do—playing for the enjoyment of people in his own young age group. Moreover, his peers, musicians from other bands playing at other places around the lake, came to hear his large group and proclaimed it comparable to the one led by the already-famous Stan Kenton.

The group was billed as "The Band That Jumps" and its theme song, written by Bob Kaywoodie, who also did the arranging for the band, was "Danger, Men Blasting!" And, except when restrained by Globini, they did.

Back at school, the Brubeck big band worked a number of gigs as a unit, including end-of-the-week sessions at Stockton's Memorial Auditorium, where all the big recording bands also appeared. Dave also worked on occasion as a solo pianist. In one instance, the operator of a Carson City, Nevada, joint, having taken one look at Dave's profile, billed him, to Dave's considerable chagrin, as "The Only Indian Jazz Pianist in Captivity."

There was the *Friday Frolics*, a weekly, Friday afternoon student variety show, broadcast (only on campus) over the COP five-watt radio station. Dave and a rhythm section played everything from cue music to featured instrumentals. It was an ambitious undertaking, and a key participant was Iola Whitlock.

Friday Frolics was, by all reports, the *Big Show* of closed-circuit radio, a grand training ground for all concerned, but its place in history is assured as the place where Dave Brubeck met his wife-to-be.

Dave, in those days, was heavy on the foot-tapping. He remembers that he had just taken his shoes off prior to a broadcast and was shaking the coins and keys from his pockets into the shoes to minimize distracting noise when he played. Iola, who was that day the show's director, came into the studio. "She said that was the first time she'd ever seen a piano player who had to take his shoes off to play piano, a rather strange thing to do. All I could think to say was, 'I've been kicked out of better places than this!'" Not the most promising exchange for what was to become a lasting romance.

As Iola recalls, the show had a singer named Louise Anton, Dave and rhythm, and a substantial cast of characters for the comedy sketches. "One week I would be the director and the next week I'd be in the sketches. Dave likes to say I played 'Mag the Hag,' but I played other parts as well." The one-hour weekly production was a

     CHAPTER TWO

learning arena for a number of students who went on to distinguished careers in and out of show business. Comedian Bud Stefan eventually directed his talents and energy into becoming a major force in advertising. Darren McGavin, Barbara Baxley, and Jo Van Fleet, all from the COP drama department, became well known in films and on the stage. Jack Toomay became a specialist in radar and rose to a very high rank in the military. For Iola, this all-around training, from sound effects to continuity, from acting to directing, led to roles on radio network drama and to writing lyrics for some of Dave's major compositions.

Iola, often called Olie by Dave and close friends, was born in Corning ("The Olive Capital of the World"), near Red Bluff, California. Her earliest years were spent in the tiny town of Chrome in the foothills of the Coast Range. This was followed by a move to Willows and grade school, and then to Redding, on the eastern edge of the Trinity Alps.

Her father worked for the Forest Service, and neither parent had much interest in the arts. Her mother had grown up on various ranches near such remote spots as Peanut and Hayfork, between Red Bluff and Eureka. Her family, like Dave's on his father's side, had been in ranching in California for many decades.

Both Iola and Dave, reared in such rural environments, went on to become sophisticated travelers and international celebrities, but the early influences—love of and insistence on closeness of family, self-resourcefulness, a steady devotion to basic values—were deeply ingrained in both and certainly contributed to the signal success of their marriage. Each was to reinforce the other. It's arguable that Dave would never have known the success he achieved without the rock-steady support, inspiration, and good sense of Iola.

At Shasta Union High School in Redding, which was then a boom town spurred by the construction of Shasta Dam, Iola got caught up in drama and in debate and speech contests, several of which she won. After graduation as valedictorian of her class in 1940, she opted to attend first the junior college in Stockton (where her parents had moved) and then the upper division classes at the private College of the Pacific, just as Dave was doing. "I enrolled as a speech major, but I was also interested in drama, and so I did both. Then, when I went into the upper division, they offered a degree in radio. It was about the only school west of the Mississippi that offered such a degree. That became my major in Senior College." Her teachers included John Crabbe in radio and DeMarcus Brown in drama. *Friday Frolics* was part of the radio curriculum.

Neither Dave nor Iola paid much attention to each other during their first contact on the *Frolics* show. It fell to Harold Meeske, the guitarist on the show, to really bring the pair together. Dave remembers that he told Harold, his roommate at the time, "'Harold, I've got to go to one college fraternity function, my parents insist on it. Who's the smartest girl at the College of Pacific?' He said, 'Iola Whitlock.' I asked if he thought I could get a date with her, and he agreed to try to arrange that. He did, and when I got back the night of our first date, Harold asked how it went. I said, 'We're gonna get married.'"

Dave graduated in June, and they dated all that summer of 1942. Then Dave joined the army. On a brief leave, he and Iola were married in Carson City, Nevada, on September 21 in a religious ceremony in a church with only the minister and his wife present. Their wedding night was spent up the road in Lake Tahoe, right by Stateline, near Dave's old haunt of Globin's. One night was all they had, for Dave had to report back for duty at Camp Haan at Riverside, just east of Los Angeles.

At first, Iola returned to her parents' home in Stockton to finish up the college term. Upon finishing college, she moved to Riverside to be near Dave, who also spent time at Camp Irwin in the desert near Barstow. She managed to land a job at a local radio station, KPRO, then owned by Dr. E. L. Laisne, an optometrist who used his station and others all around the state to plug his optometry business. Iola says, "I did everything. Everything from writing ads to pulling records, writing the announcer's copy. I did the log, some news editing, and once in a while I was on the air myself. KPRO is where I learned most about jazz, I think, because whoever had preceded me as music director had a wonderful collection of jazz records. The announcers who worked as disc jockeys really knew nothing about it, so I had free reign to pull whatever I wanted to hear and write them little announcements about it."

As war-time needs for manpower increased, Dave was shipped overseas. Iola gradually got into big-time radio in Hollywood, joined

American Federation of Radio Artists and got a running part on Mutual's *Red Ryder* adventure series, out of the old KHJ, playing a rough pioneer character called "Kate." She also did many free-lance parts on various radio shows.

Like many musicians who enlisted in the service in 1942, Dave, after auditioning, was initially assigned to a band. In his case, it was at Riverside's Camp Haan, where his old friend, Ernie Farmer, was also stationed. This assignment lasted for about two years, not only giving Dave off-duty time to be with his wife, but also allowing him to visit Los Angeles and attempt to ignite some sparks for a future career.

Stan Kenton dominated the big band scene in Southern California and was to go national in a big way when the recording ban of the time was finally resolved and Capitol Records turned out his early hits. Dave took it upon himself to write a piece called "Prayer of the Conquered" for Kenton and managed to finally see Stan and play the rather ambitious composition for him. Stan liked it well enough to run down the arrangement at an NBC rehearsal, but found Brubeck even ahead of his own fairly avant-garde approach. Dave says Stan told him to come back in ten years.

Dave also wangled an introduction to a much-feared and admired composer, Arnold Schoenberg, then teaching at UCLA. There was an interview and one lesson. Schoenberg's approach was pedantic and uncompromising. Dave's was searching, experimental, visceral. It was not a happy pairing of teacher and student.

But Dave was not to spend the entire war playing piano in Riverside, California. "In 1944, when D-day was coming up, they busted the whole band and put us in the infantry," Dave remembers. "I was assigned to go overseas as a rifleman. When they got to the point they were about to ship me out, I told the lieutenant in charge that I had never had basic training. He said, 'This is impossible. How long have you been in the army?' I said, 'Two years.' He looked up my records and saw I wasn't lying. So he said, 'I'm gonna give you basic training and get you on that ship. Any training that's going on in this camp you gotta do until you're qualified.' It was a personal crusade. Night and day he'd be waking me up, and I'd be out there throwing hand grenades, shooting a BAR [Browning Automatic Rifle], digging trenches. It seemed like it'd never end."

But it did, and Dave was on his way. Prior to being shipped to the East Coast and overseas, Dave went to San Francisco on leave, where his old roommate, Dave Van Kriedt, was playing in the 253rd Infantry band, stationed at the Presidio. Van Kriedt, suggested that Dave meet the other members of the band and sit in for a tune or two. Among those players was a thin, bespectacled clarinetist and sometime alto player named Paul Breitenfeld, who later changed his name to Paul Desmond. This chance encounter, during which Paul was both amused and amazed by Dave's approach to harmony and poly-tonality, was to make a profound change in the lives and careers of both men a few years later.

Time for War

Sudden twists of fate. Chance meetings. Sheer luck. For many an American fighting man during World War II, these random factors determined life or death. For Rifleman Dave Brubeck, a qualified sharpshooter but no gung-ho, battle-tested soldier, it seemed luck was running against him ninety days after the D-day invasion of Europe on June 6, 1944. Like many in the American contingent of the 176,000-man force that crossed the channel at night to begin the final chapter of what Studs Terkel has called the "Good War," Dave had landed at Omaha Beach. From there a troop train had taken the group of replacement soldiers to a switching point at Verdun.

Dave remembers, "If the train turned left, we'd be in Omar Bradley's army, up near Belgium. We'd be fighting in Patton's army if it turned right that night. The train turned right and our hearts all sank." Patton's reputation as the toughest of the tough guys had by then been established.

As it happened, the cattle-car troop train deposited Dave and his fellow soldiers in what Dave remembers only as the "Mud Hole." There was mud, mud, and more mud as far as the eye could see.

They ate in it, slept in it, and waited for orders to move to the front in it. A total surprise was the arrival of a Red Cross troupe bent on giving the GIs some small relief from their grim surroundings and uncertain future. They traveled with a piano and when they asked, "Can anyone here play the piano?" Dave volunteered. It was his first opportunity to make music since leaving the States, and he made the most of it. But his big break was yet to come, and because of it, Brubeck was to remain at the fringe of combat during most of the rest of the war. He was never called to the front as a rifleman. For this he can thank an officer whose name was Leroy Pearlman.

Dave was a replacement in Patton's Third Army, 140th Regiment, A Company. Pearlman was in Patton's army too, having come to Normandy on D-day plus twenty. He was one of the most colorful characters among the many mavericks who managed to maneuver and con their way through the thicket of majors and colonels and GI red tape that defeated those who were short on chuztpah. Pearlman had been drafted before the United States entered the war, after having done everything from selling roses in Manhattan subway stations to acting in the Chicago Repertory Company.

In Chicago, Pearlman met Studs Terkel, the opera and sports buff, author, and, as the years went by, noted interviewer and story-teller. Terkel eventually wrote of Pearlman's exploits in three of his books. When it came to *The Good War* (1984), Pearlman had decided that his current position as stockbroker didn't blend well with his earlier careers, so he contrived a pseudonym, Ray Wax. Studs used that name in a much-quoted chapter titled "Sudden Money" and thereby totally confused Dave and others who quoted from Terkel's otherwise accurate account. It wasn't until late in the research for this book that the real identity of the mysterious Ray Wax was discovered to be Leroy Pearlman.

Here's how Pearlman remembered the story in 1993, almost fifty years after it happened. "Nothing much was being done in the way of rehabilitation or entertainment for the troops returning to just outside the battle lines with battle fatigue. I had already managed to come up with shadow boxes made of discarded crates left on the beaches. I showed films with them. Then I made a portable stage out of prefab sections of flooring the Germans had left behind. Now came the first of the USO shows, starring Dinah Shore, who was great. About then, as we were following Patton's troops, we wound up in a little town outside Fontainebleau, called Malesherbes. We were living in one of the Vanderbilt châteaux that had a collection of rare dolls and a moat. I went out of my mind. I had libraries set up. I had people swimming in the moat. I had tours running in the château until the guys started to steal the dolls.

"By this time," he continued, "I was flying so high you had to go through a sergeant to talk to me. And a guy did come to talk. He said he played the sax, and he had a piano player and a couple of other guys and could they set up a band. So I turned to the piano player and asked him his name. He said, 'Dave Brubeck.' I said, 'How do you play, modern?' He said, 'Yes.' I was fishing, so I said, 'Like Kenton?' And he said, 'Well, something like Kenton.'"

Pearlman was in a unique position. He literally had the power of life and death over people. "The army picked the replacements to go forward through a kind of punch-card system, part of what was called a Form 20. The way I was able to build a band was to pull all the Form 20s for the sixteen or eighteen guys we needed. In other words, they just disappeared from the records. No one could move them. Naturally, the man who gravitated to the top to lead the band was Dave Brubeck."

The paperwork's disappearance had unexpected repercussions. First, Dave's mother's closest friend had a letter she had written to Dave in Germany returned, marked "deceased." Then Iola got a letter from an army department asking, "Can you give us information about where your husband is?" Meanwhile, Dave's mother's friend had fortunately said nothing about the "deceased" stamp on her returned letter because Iola continued to receive letters from Dave. Thus the family knew he was alive, even though he wasn't allowed to write anything that might hint of his whereabouts or his activities. It was a long, confusing time before the folks back home learned that Dave was leading a band, facing friendly GIs, not hostile Germans.

Pearlman says the band was officially known as the Jazz Band with the Third Army Replacement Depot. Dave remembers that it had a nickname, the Wolf Pack. He doesn't remember who came up with the name or why. But he'll never forget that this lucky break and Captain Pearlman's audacity probably saved his life by removing him from the replacement pool on the eve of what turned out to be a very dangerous action.

"The command had brought up some huge cannon on the railroad to try to blast the Germans out of an emplacement on a hill," says Dave. "The Germans were in a position to start shelling. The only way they could get them down was to send replacements up there and dump oil in their bunkers. That meant our guys had to go right up the mountain at point-blank range and dump the oil and light it. That's where I think I was going. Some guys I never heard from again were in on that, where I would have been that day."

Instead, Dave and the band formed a nucleus of musicians and entertainers that would spend the rest of the war together. With Pearlman's jerry-built portable stage and a truck he had conned out of a friendly general, they brought to the weary soldiers the relief that any army needs: music and laughter.

About the band, Pearlman says, "They had free movement. They didn't have to report to formation; they didn't have to answer to any officer except, in theory, me. I never made any demands on them except that they stay out of trouble."

"Free movement" and "staying out of trouble" sometimes were incompatible. Once during a lull in activities, Pearlman told the band to "get lost," not wanting their idleness to be noticed. The band had Pearlman's appropriated truck, so they decided to do some touring. Unfortunately, they drove right into what later (mid-December 1944) became part of the Battle of the Bulge. They saw some American GIs in a clearing, eating, and thought they'd go play for them. About that time, aircraft flew overhead. They suddenly realized that these were German planes. Dave said, "Let's get the hell out of here."

The driver then made a wrong turn, which took them through enemy lines. Night had fallen, but they traveled with no headlights and had gotten past an MP before they realized he was a German MP. They drove on a little way, now knowing they were going deeper into hostile territory but not sure what to do. Finally, they turned around and sped past the MP as fast as they could, expecting every moment to be blown to bits.

Eventually the terrified musicians got back to a sentry on the eastern side of the American lines. Dave remembers, "This soldier comes up to us carrying hand grenades with the pins pulled. One of our guys kept yelling, 'Don't forget the password!' I gave it OK, but this soldier was still suspicious. It turned out that this same night, Germans wearing American uniforms, driving American trucks, had killed all of his buddies at this very spot. Luckily, we finally convinced him who we were."

Dave Brubeck was a lowly private first class, outranked by every other member of the band. Nonetheless, he was the man in charge, with a special classification of "bandleader." He later refused a warrant officer's rating because he would have had to live with the officers. He stayed with the band, which was racially integrated, an unusual situation in the American military of the time. There were Black soldiers and White soldiers, and there were Black units and White units, but the Wolf Pack was one unit, one band. It had a Black trombonist, Jonathan "Dick" Flowers, and a Black emcee, Gil White, together with a White leader and the other members of the band of which the majority was White.

Some of the musicians had suffered battle injuries. Their musical abilities had been discovered in their hospital recovery units and they were identified as musicians. They were sent to Brubeck, who put them in the band. Many in the GI audiences were made more comfortable by the Purple Hearts that these band members wore when they played. Performances were often given right at the front. Dave says, "I remember when we'd be playing a show, and the German planes would come in to strafe, and every available gun was used to try to shoot them down."

The Wolf Pack played with many a visiting celebrity. The band included some exceptional entertainers of its own, like comedian Johnny Stanley and songwriter Leon Pober.

Leroy Pearlman says, "When winter came, we went to live on the Maginot Line in a little town called Neufchâteau. I grabbed a little hotel, the Moderne, and set up an officer's bar. The town had a theater, and I asked Brubeck to put together a show to entertain the citizens. They packed the place. They hung from the rafters. And Brubeck played really wild with that sixteen-piece band. Of course, we played a lot of shows, one with Marlene Dietrich. That was wild, too!"

Dave lived all by himself in the town theater, while the band members lived in an old castle that the Germans had occupied. Dave remembers the castle: "There was a well in the middle of it. You went down the equivalent of three or four stories to reach it, but that well had been very important in the siege days because it gave the castle its own source of water."

He remembers another little town on the Maginot Line, where the band was billeted during that winter of 1944–45. It was Thionville. "The officers were on the first two floors of this big, old building, and we were in the basement on a dirt floor. We were glad to be there, out of the cold. The furnace that heated the whole building was down there. On nights when we got strafed, the officers came down and joined us. Of course we could just stay right in bed. We returned there during the Battle of the Bulge, listening to Axis Sally on the radio telling us to 'come out with your hands up!'"

At this time, General Patton was stalled about seventy-five miles north and east of Neufchâteau, just below Metz, waiting for gasoline so his army could move on. When it came, he broke through Metz and kept going into Germany, with the band right behind him. "Finally, we got to Nuremburg," remembers Pearlman. "I raced to try to get the opera house. This was about six days after the Third Army took the city and went on to Munich." After some hassle, Pearlman got half of the hall, which had a large hole in the roof but was otherwise intact, complete with Hitler's box and Goebbel's box. The band went right along. There were some extraordinary shows, including one with Alfred Lunt and Lynn Fontaine.

By now it was May 1945. V-E Day came on May 7. The Rockettes arrived from New York for a postwar tour, and the top brass wanted the band to play for these famous precision dancers as they performed for the occupying troops. This was an obvious break for Brubeck and company, and Pearlman let them go, returning the purloined Form 20s. They had been together since late August of the previous year, when Paris was liberated.

Many years later, Dave was playing at the Downbeat in New York. Pearlman was a Manhattan businessman. "I went down with my wife to see him," Pearlman recalls. "He'd just begun to really make a name for himself. I walked up the aisle between sets and said, 'Hello, Dave.' He said, 'Hello, Pearlman.' There was no big, joyous, surprised reunion. That was how personally close we were. Yet, I couldn't have done any more for him than I did, and he couldn't

CHAPTER THREE

have done any more for me than he did. I was so busy fighting my major and keeping the goodwill of my colonel that I was lost in my own world during those nine months or so we were together."

Now the Wolf Pack went from battlefields and sleeping in haystacks and mud to real proscenium stages and hotels with real beds. They played in a major ski resort that had become a rest area. This was on Lake Eibse in the Bavarian Alps, north of Munich. Brubeck and the band spent the better part of the next six months there and in other parts of Germany, playing for the occupation troops. They still had no access to army musical instruments. They had to get better equipment by bartering with cigarettes as they toured through German towns and, later, in Czechoslovakian areas known for instrument making.

As lucky as Dave Brubeck had been, as favored by good twists of fate and chance meetings, the war brought more than the good fortune of being able to play music for the duration. Dave still grieves for the loss of friends in battles no longer remembered by many except those who fought them. He stays in touch with many who survived. The war meant separation from Iola. Married on a three-day pass, they had spent most of their first few years apart. The war years may partly account for their unrelenting companionship ever since.

After the war in Europe had been won, Dave faced reassignment to the Pacific, and the renewed threat of death on the battlefield. That threat ended with the dropping of the atomic bomb. To this day, the double significance of the bomb troubles him: relief that he and tens of thousands of youngsters had been spared when Japan surrendered and grief at the immeasurable disaster inflicted by the nuclear weapons.

The war also showed Dave just how much music mattered in his life. Discharged in 1946, he left the Wolf Pack behind and headed back to California for more academic study, determined to get his still-evolving, polytonal, polyrhythm but not-bop music accepted in the jazz community and to make it a part of the American musical mainstream. It had saved his life. Music would be his life from that time forward.

Time for
New Beginnings

In 1946, Mills College in Oakland, California, was an all-female school, modeled on Vassar and Radcliffe in the East. It had an advanced faculty and a pronounced affinity for exploring the arts and, in particular, music's new meanings for a postwar world.

At war's end, with the flood of returning servicemen, the college opened its doors to a few male music students. Among them, in the fall of 1946 and spring of 1947 were Dave Brubeck, Bill Smith, Jack Weeks, Dave Van Kriedt, and Dick Collins—five of the eight instrumentalists who would make up the Octet. Pianist Brubeck and clarinetist Smith met on the Mills campus and a fusion of talent took place almost instantaneously.

The catalyst was Darius Milhaud, whose avant-garde classical compositions had made him one of France's most celebrated musical figures in the 1930s. The war forced him to seek sanctuary in the United States, and Mills College offered him a position on their music faculty.

It was Milhaud's appreciation of jazz that attracted Brubeck and Smith. Dave's chord structures were already set in tight intervals; he was already experimenting with polyrhythms. "My brother was Milhaud's assistant," Dave says. "I had seen Milhaud before I left. If I survived the war, I knew the first thing I was going to do was go study with him because he understood me.

"I had one or two teachers at the College of the Pacific who were very encouraging, but Milhaud was by far the *most* encouraging. Most other teachers were not interested in jazz, as I was. I was also interested in composition and counterpoint. I never played classical piano. Most everything I learned was through osmosis—whether it was through Milhaud or my mother."

Brubeck and his cohorts weren't the first men to study composition and theory with Milhaud. In fact, Brubeck's brother Howard was one of the first two male graduate students admitted to Mills to study with Milhaud; pianist and arranger Pete Rugolo was the other.

Studying with Milhaud was a combination of private lessons and group sessions that left an indelible mark on Dave Brubeck's music and his heart. "I would have to struggle so hard to write down what I was thinking. I wasn't technically equipped to do it, but Milhaud would always be reassuring. Eventually I would be able to get something down. I orchestrated for the Octet things that we never performed, like parts of Milhaud's jazz-oriented ballet, 'Creation of the World.'"

Bill Smith remembers Brubeck in those days, "He played chords you wouldn't believe. It was astounding. His harmonic sense was so far advanced, it was shocking."

At first just a nameless group of eight musicians began to play together—studying, composing, and arranging, not believing that they were destined for anything special but all eager to hear the new sounds on the pages they had written. There was no leader. The group played for friends, played a benefit, and played for each other and, in time, became a forerunner of the small jazz groups Brubeck has headed for almost the next half-century. As Smith says, "It just sort of fell together. I was in class with Dave. I used to read Bartok violin duets with Dick Collins; he on the trumpet and I on the clarinet, and so we played together. Jack Weeks, who was also in the class, played trombone and bass, and so to make use of his talents was obvious. Dave Van Kriedt was in the class playing tenor sax. There was one other horn—alto—Paul Desmond. He wasn't in the composition class, but he was a good friend.

"That was the horn section. It wasn't much more at first than a rehearsal band. Just eight guys who got together and played because we wanted to hear what we were writing sounded like, and we were good friends."

Dave says Milhaud suggested that members of the Octet write their fugue and counterpoint assignments for their jazz instruments. When the results proved pleasing, Milhaud asked, "Would you play for the Mills women's assembly?" Dave says that the group's performance went over very well, "We were together three years."

Influenced heavily by new twentieth-century harmonies and rhythmic complexities from Europe, Africa, and Asia, Dave explored their possibilities in jazz. Polytonality, counterpoint, polyrhythm— these aspects found their way into the student work of a man whose musical message went beyond what was acceptable in most contemporary jazz settings in 1946.

At this point in American musical history, seminal changes were underway. The big band era was coming to an early close. The musicians recording strike of 1942 to 1944 had been deadly for those name bands whose leaders hadn't enlisted or been drafted. New recording stopped (except on V-Discs for the armed forces only). Such band singers as Frank Sinatra and Dick Haymes had gone out on their own, and the recording companies discovered they could get by without instruments, using a cappella backups on the vocalists' records. The era of the singers had begun, and the returning servicemen soon became ardent fans. While band leaders such as Duke Ellington and Woody Herman managed to survive, often by replacing whole sections of drafted sidemen, and to even progress musically, it was the small groups in the tiny, smoky jazz rooms that were making revolutionary music.

What came to be known as bebop incubated in the East, but it was by 1945 invading Los Angeles with a vengeance. Norman Granz, with his first "Jazz at the Philharmonic" concert there on July 2, 1944, featuring Illinois Jacquet, J. J. Johnson, Nat King Cole, and guitarist Les Paul, had begun an enormously influential series that survived, with some interruptions, until 1967. The trumpet player Howard McGhee, along with pianist Sir Charles Thompson, bassist Oscar

Pettiford, and drummer Denzil Best had come west with Coleman Hawkins, whose tenor, while not in the bebop groove, was showing distinctly modern traces. Then Charlie Parker and Dizzy Gillespie opened at Billy Berg's in Hollywood in December of 1945. That event shook jazz concepts held by many musicians to the foundations, while passing almost unnoticed among the general public. Innovators such as Dodo Marmarosa, Teddy Edwards, and Miles Davis began to be heard in a variety of Los Angeles venues and on record labels like Dial and Savoy.

It's worth noting that Dave Brubeck up in San Francisco was paying little attention to all this music in Southern California, which may explain why he never became a bop player and why he and Paul Desmond (also mainstream, in his playing) worked so well together in later years.

Looking back in early 1995, Dave said, "I was in a period when I was trying not to listen to much jazz. I was trying to develop an individual style. I probably heard Miles Davis's 'Birth of the Cool' once, maybe at Dave Van Kriedt's place, but as far as owning jazz records of the time or trying to listen and be influenced, that didn't happen. If any contemporary jazz player impressed me it was George Shearing. In fact, I once told *Down Beat* magazine that it was Shearing who made it possible for jazz people to start working again, right across the United States." Brubeck was clearly referring to the fact that the general public was turned off, rather than on, by bebop, big band or small band, while remaining open to other innovations in jazz such as Dave's ventures into meters and polytonality. Remember that these experiments remained melody based and swing oriented.

The original Brubeck Octet did jar some listeners while intriguing others. Dave's father, hearing a performance at College of the Pacific, reported to a newspaper critic, "That was the damnedest bunch of noise I've ever heard."

That the musicians and composers in the group were all in one place at one time was one of those occurrences that cannot be explained, except for the presence of Milhaud. The French composer remained at Mills for another two years. Then he went home, but for a long time thereafter alternated his teaching years between Mills College and the Paris Conservatoire. By that time, he had influenced the face of jazz in the United States. There would be no turning back.

The Octet played for music, not for money. It was playing music that was "weird," as some observers put it. Smith laughingly recalls that a rare booking in a Chinese restaurant lasted until the owners heard the music. And, if Chinese cuisine did not harmonize with the Octet's music, neither did any other commercial enterprise. A couple of College of the Pacific bookings plus two public concerts were the only paying gigs the Octet could get in three years.

In desperation, Dave, by then supporting a wife and two young children by playing casuals, took a steady job with a combo called The Three D's: Dave, Don, and Darrell—Brubeck on piano, Don Ratto on bass, Darrell Cutler on tenor sax and sock cymbal. Frances Lynn was the vocalist; Darrell was the leader.

"We played six nights a week in the Geary Cellar, under the Geary Theater in San Francisco. It lasted a year or more. It was a good paying job: we got a hundred dollars each a week. I was lucky—a lot of guys didn't have a steady job."

There was a lot of exposure as well. Players in major bands coming through San Francisco would make the Cellar a regular stop after their own performances. The Brubeck name was becoming known. What the musicians were hearing were advanced harmonies and the beginnings of Brubeck's innovations with time signatures. Before Miles Davis, Brubeck was scoring in 6/4 time, and Bill Smith in 7 and 5.

A recording exists of an early jazz variation, a piece called "Curtain Music," a scant thirty-three seconds of jazz played by the Octet as a signature theme for its Mills College assembly performances. The 6/4 tempo carries signs of the music that would later capture Broadway in Leonard Bernstein's *West Side Story* score, contrapuntal lines between piano and saxophones.

This 1946 acetate was chosen to lead off Columbia's Legacy Brubeck collection, *Time Signatures, A Career Retrospective*. This selection was an appropriate choice: it was the first Brubeck recording of hundreds that would follow as Dave blazed a trail into the future of jazz. With Cal Tjader and Ron Crotty, he was playing 6/4 in versions of "Singin' in the Rain," an early departure from the standard 4/4 beat that typified pop music and especially, jazz.

Dave then tried a jazz waltz tempo. "It drove the rhythm sections crazy," he says. "But I wanted to play *against* the rhythm sections rather than with them, just as a modern choreographer does in ballet. You see, people weren't ready for the concept of superimposing, which was harmonically and rhythmically what I wanted to do. People just wanted to play like a European march, but syncopated, which was basically New Orleans jazz. They wanted to stay there. African music was full of superimposing different beats one on top of the other. Many in the jazz community had not heard real African music. Musicians and critics would look at me like I was crazy. I would say, 'If you're trying to reflect Africa, you're not doing it.' They'd say, 'It doesn't swing unless it's in 4/4 time.' It was very hard to get a rhythm section to do what I wanted it to do."

It was a rough and uncompromising path for the pianist-composer who was emerging more and more as a prophet of a different time concept, an identifiable new sound that was based as much in rhythm as it was in melody.

It was also a rough time for the Brubeck family purse. Just as The Three D's was getting a following—albeit one made up mostly of musicians—disaster struck.

Paul Desmond was in the habit of dropping by and "sitting in" with the group. One day Desmond got a chance to be a leader on his own at a Quonset hut kind of place called the Band Box, down Highway 101 near Stanford University. He raided The Three D's, taking Norman Bates, who by then had become the bass player, as well as singer Frances Lynn. Dave says, "All of a sudden there wasn't a group anymore, so I went along, too. I went from a hundred a week to the forty-two Paul offered me. I didn't know how the hell I was going to live on the money, but I knew the music would be good."

Paul used to drive Dave the thirty miles down to Palo Alto at what Dave remembers as ninety miles an hour, making every stoplight (they were set for forty-five miles per hour), breaking every traffic law. He says he never expected to live through the next ride. It was Panicsville for the Brubecks, with Iola haunting the markets to save pennies and Dave fearing for his life during the nightly commute, but still, Dave enjoyed every moment of the playing with Desmond.

Then Paul was offered another job, up on the Feather River in the Sierras, hot and dry in the summer, wet and green in the winter. He promptly quit the Band Box, took Frances Lynn and Norman Bates, hired another piano player, and left Brubeck stranded. "It was an unforgivable thing he did," Dave remembers with obvious pain. And, he told Gene Lees, "I said, 'Paul, OK, I'm going to bring Bill Smith in on clarinet because the guy at the Band Box said he will keep me on.' He said, 'No! It's my job!' He wouldn't let me take the job. He got furious. He said, 'I found this job; it's my job when I come back!' He was going to the Feather River Inn for three months." Desmond did not come back. He joined Alvino Rey as lead alto when the summer was over.

Dave was out in the cold. He told Iola, "I *never* want to see Paul Desmond again." He did land another job. "I wound up playing with Rudy Salvini at Al Davis's Silver Log Tavern in Clearlake, up in the coastal mountains above Santa Rosa. That was forty-two fifty a week, and two meals for me, and a room with a tin roof and *no windows*, about nine by nine. It was an oven. My whole family was there. We had to spend the day at the lake. My young son Darius would just float in the water. We'd buy a picnic lunch. At night we got sacks and dipped them in tubs of water and ran a fan to cool the place. Sometimes we slept on the open porch until daylight."

The ordeal ended when a phone call came from Jimmy Lyons offering a job at the Burma Lounge at Lake Merritt in Oakland. Lyons asked for a trio: Brubeck, Cal Tjader, and Ron Crotty. Dave couldn't accept fast enough. Lyons was the very influential host of a late-night KNBC radio show (midnight to 2:00 A.M.). He had first met Brubeck when Dave was the pianist with The Three D's in the Geary Theater basement. Lyons was to become one of Brubeck's earliest and most dedicated supporters—an unflagging promoter, using the power of his radio shows on KNBC and other Bay Area stations to air Brubeck recordings and to find paying gigs for the then little-known pianist.

Jimmy Lyons' career as broadcaster, promoter, friend, and mentor to generations of people in the jazz world invites comparison with the career of John Hammond and merits a closer look. He had done the earliest Stan Kenton remote broadcasts in 1941 from the Rendezvous Ballroom at Balboa Beach in Southern California.

These, together with a series of radio transcriptions also voiced by Jimmy and produced by the legendary C. P. MacGregor studios in Los Angeles, spread the exciting sound of the new Kenton band all over the nation. The sixteen-inch, radio-station-only disks were recorded with an audience of musicians' families and fans applauding after each take. The sessions remain available today on Hindsight Records as a testament to the exuberance of Kenton, his men, and the emotion-charged young announcer.

Lyons, working later that year for NBC in New York, was drafted. But, through the intervention of Joe Thompson, an NBC producer about to depart for a South Pacific posting with the Armed Forces Radio Service (AFRS), Jimmy lucked into an AFRS job in Hollywood. There he did the now-famous *Jubilee* shows, beamed all over the world by shortwave and transcriptions played on AFRS stations in jungles, deserts, and edge-of-war outposts everywhere. Every jazz artist available, Black and White, appeared on the shows. Many became lifelong friends of Lyons, making possible the Monterey Jazz Festivals, which Jimmy began in 1958. Dave Brubeck appeared in the first and last concerts Jimmy produced there.

Lyons' third wife, Laurel, had actually known Dave far earlier. Her father had run the Moffat family ranches in Nevada, while Dave's father had managed similar spreads in California. As a child, Laurel frequently visited the Brubecks in Ione. Thus, she was as supportive of Brubeck as Jimmy was when the chances to further Brubeck's career came along.

When Jimmy Lyons had a heart attack and was summarily dismissed as the director of the Monterey Jazz Festival in 1992, the Lyons's found themselves with little income. A year before Jimmy died, they were forced to move from their beloved apartment overlooking San Francisco Bay to a much less expensive place in Morro Bay. Dave immediately proposed a benefit concert, which he would organize, in which all performers (each one a long-time friend of Jimmy's and participant in many a festival event) would play without compensation. Although the concert never materialized, Dave's obvious affection for Jimmy and gratitude for his support over more than forty years were clearly demonstrated.

Lyons' first important contribution to Brubeck's career was that 1949 job at Oakland's Burma Lounge. It was a major turn in the fortunes of the Trio. It didn't, however, end Dave's bitterness toward Paul.

Iola had these instructions: "If Paul Desmond comes back, don't let him in the door." And Desmond did come back, one day, having heard a Trio recording on the radio in New York City while touring with Alvino Rey. He found the Brubecks and knocked on the door, which was answered by Iola. Dave was on the back porch hanging out diapers. Talking to Gene Lees, Iola remembered, "I went out back and told Dave, 'You just have to see him.' Paul was all charm, and full of promises to Dave. He said, 'If you'll just let me play with you, I'll baby-sit, I'll wash your car.'" Dave's resistance, of course, crumbled, and in the end, the two worked together for more than seventeen years.

Paul never apologized, never explained why he had left; he only begged to be let back in. And it was not the last time this mercurial, moody musician would disappear from and then reappear in the Brubeck organization.

Meanwhile, Dave, Cal, and Ron were beginning to make waves at the Burma Lounge. More and more young piano players came by to catch the new sounds coming from, in particular, the guy at the keyboard. One of the audience was an up-and-coming young automobile dealer named Carl Jefferson, who probably gained inspiration from these sessions for his later spectacular career as owner of Concord Jazz Records and founder of the Concord Jazz Festival.

"I was just fascinated by the music," Jefferson remembered. "It was so *different.* I had been a jazz junkie before that—I hung out at the jazz clubs in San Francisco when I was seventeen or eighteen. We had some great ones, like the Club Alabam' at Post and Fillmore. I'd sneak in to hear Art Tatum and people like that. But Dave's music sort of transcended jazz. The wonderful thing he did, he got a lot of people to cross over from whatever they were musically into—what they thought was jazz—and they liked it. That's why 'Take Five' was the first million-seller in jazz all those years later. It broadened the market for all of us. Dave was and is a great addition to the music scene, both musically and morally. He set a standard for everybody who followed." The Burma Club, with Cal Tjader and Ron Crotty, was a beginning.

It was still a long way to acceptance, however. Dave would tell ensuing drummers not to follow him when he arched over and under their rhythm, when he played 7/4 tempo in a 4/4 piece; many, accustomed to playing with the piano or lead instrument could not follow his idea of counterpoint. One told him: "Brubeck, you don't want a drummer, you want a machine."

"I didn't want a machine," Dave says. "I wanted polyrhythm, where a guy would stay where he was and then I would play over him or against him in another rhythm. Most of the time I'd come back way down the road, and I'd say, 'Just be there when I get there.' They would often get lost."

There were other pioneers on the musical scene: Boyd Raeburn was organizing bands with instruments usually reserved for symphonic orchestras, playing music that owed more to Stravinksy than to Tin Pan Alley. Stan Kenton's powerhouse music was blowing people's hair straight back, pouring out volumes of sound and crashing chords that explored a new dimension in sheer acoustic limits.

Like them, the Octet played arranged scores, the work of its own members usually, but it also left room for instrumental soloists and improvisations. The jazz idiom was retained, maintained, and encouraged amid scores that included fugues, preludes, dances from ballets, complex counterpoint, and dissonant chords with ever-tighter intervals. There was a sense of urgency in the music that was clearly tied to the new American social structure. The postwar years were full of production, capacity, appetite for innovation, competition among emerging entrepreneurs: the war had changed a nation that had been agricultural and industrial into a commercial arsenal seeking new ways to conquer new worlds.

It needed new anthems for its march into the second half of the twentieth century. But music was not a place to get rich, then. Brubeck, with a young wife and family, sought jobs he could get to fill the kitchen larder—often spinach for dinner and spinach soup for the next six nights—while he was trying to get his own music heard more and accepted more. There were solo gigs anywhere he could find them. He often traveled miles through the San Francisco fog to reach a club where he'd play standard music, then drive miles home after midnight to write the arrangements for the Octet when they could get a booking. The next night he'd be back on the road for another slim-paying piano gig.

Dave taught briefly, an extension course at the University of California at Berkeley, originating its history of jazz curriculum. The pay was low; the opinion of jazz among members of the university faculty was even lower. One faculty member said, when told about the new course being added to the curriculum, "I'd rather sleep with a dog than have my name in a catalog with a jazz musician." What the jazz-ignorant professor at Berkeley did not know was that the Dave Brubeck Trio—Brubeck plus the rhythm section of the Octet, Cal Tjader and Ron Crotty—would strike gold.

Three years after the Octet had put its first fragment on acetate at Mills College, Dave's trio did its first commercial recording, initially on the obscure Coronet label, later to be re-released and given far more circulation on a record label that Dave helped found and with which he was to be involved for many years: Fantasy. The label would become both a great window of opportunity and a source of considerable anguish for Dave, as events in the following chapter will show. The most immediate consequence of the Fantasy affiliation was the exposure to a growing number of listeners, via radio airings first and foremost, of the Trio's abrupt, unrepentant, arrhythmic Brubeck metaphors. *Down Beat* and *Metronome* critics voted the Trio the best new musical organization of the year; critic John Hammond lavished praise on the Brubeck style and sound.

It was 1950, halfway through the century, and the threshold of a new era in jazz music in America.

Dave Brubeck in an early, about 1927, photo at
one of his mother's pianos in Concord, California.
With Dave is older brother Howard.

Pete Brubeck, Dave's father, on his
Concord ranch in the early 1930s.

Brubeck at age sixteen, Arroyo
Seco Ranch, Ione, California.

*Twenty-two-year-old Dave Brubeck in 1942,
on the eve of becoming a husband and a
soldier, with wife-to-be, Iola Whitlock.*

Dave's first army band, The Fabulous Five,
with Brubeck on piano; Ralph Gephardt, bass;
Wes Cope, trombone; and Frances Glenn
Cope, singer, Camp Haan, California, 1942.

The Three D's, Don Ratto, Frances Lynn, Darrell Cutler, and Dave Brubeck, at the Geary Cellar, San Francisco, 1947.

Dave Brubeck Octet at the Blackhawk where they performed every Sunday, San Francisco, 1949. LEFT TO RIGHT: Bill Smith, Paul Desmond, Dave Van Kriedt, Cal Tjader, Ron Crotty, Dick Collins, Bob Collins, and Dave Brubeck.

A serious moment for the Dave Brubeck Trio,
as they try on their new, and first, "uniforms."
LEFT TO RIGHT: *Dave, bassist Ron Crotty,*
and Cal Tjader.

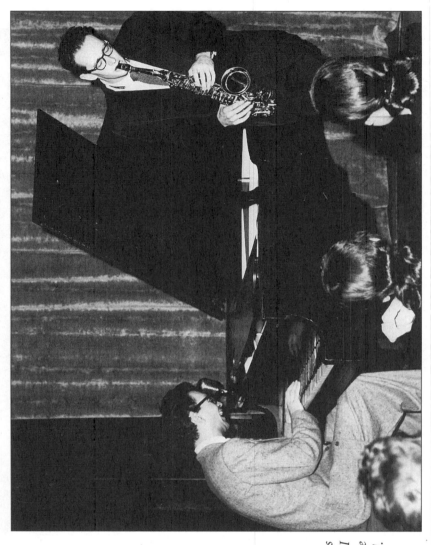

"Over the years, he was the most loyal friend I ever had." So said Dave Brubeck of Paul Desmond.

At Birdland in New York City, mid-1950s.
LEFT TO RIGHT: *Joe Dodge, drums; Bob Bates, bass;*
Dave Brubeck, piano; and Paul Desmond, alto.

A rehearsal session in New York, 1956. Paul Desmond is pondering a suggestion from Dave's brother Howard Brubeck, at right. Norman Bates is on bass, replacing his brother Bob; Joe Dodge is on drums.

Dave Brubeck and Joe Dodge
during a 1956 concert tour.

*A serious moment of introspection
with Norman Bates and Dave, 1965.*

Producer George Avakian, Columbia Records engineer Fred Plant, bassist Norman Bates, Dave, drummer Joe Morello, and Paul Desmond critique a playback, probably during Dave Digs Disney session, 1957.

The Classic Quartet on tour. Brubeck, "Senator" Eugene Wright, Paul Desmond, and Joe Morello somewhere in the world, undated.

*Dave, Paul
Desmond, Joe
Morello, and
Gene Wright
at the South
Indian School
of Karnatic
Music, India,
1958.*

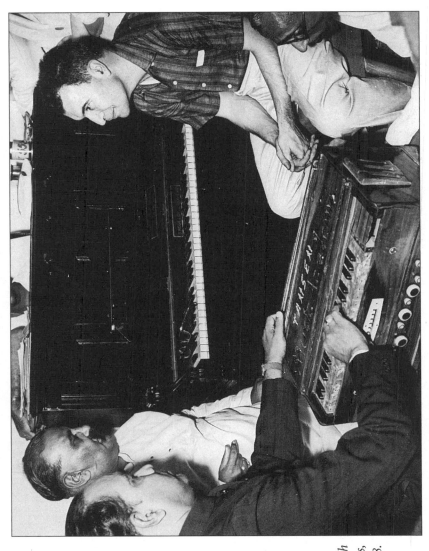

Dave conferring with Indian musicians, Bombay, 1958.

A record store in Baghdad. Brubeck is hidden by fans as he autographs his albums.

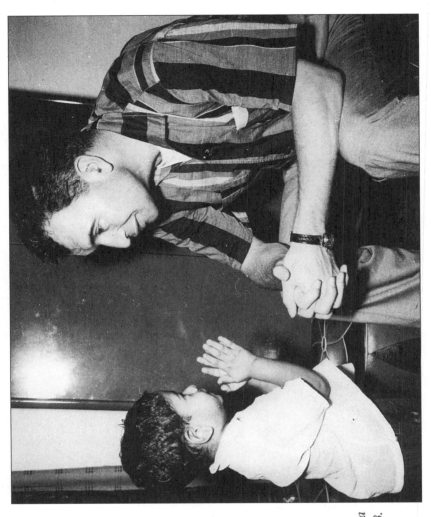

*Dave receives a critique from a
very young fan in India, 1958.*

*Paul Desmond, pleased by a playback during a
Columbia Records session in the late fifties.*

The Classic Dave Brubeck Quartet. Eugene Wright, bass; Joe Morello, drums; Paul Desmond, alto; and Dave Brubeck, piano, circa 1959–60.

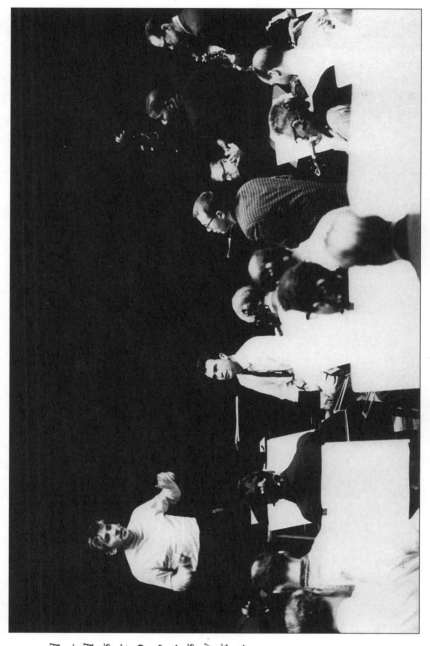

Leonard Bernstein con-
ducts Howard
Brubeck's
Dialogues for
Jazz Combo
and Orchestra,
January 30, 1960.
The Quartet is
surrounded by
the New York
Philharmonic.

Time at
Turk and Hyde

In 1949, a major epicenter for West Coast jazz opened at the corner of Turk and Hyde in San Francisco. The location became a Mecca for the young, the adventurous, and the seekers of new horizons in music. It was just a room, a "square box" as co-owner Guido Cacianti remembers it, a room that could seat maybe three hundred people, squeezed together at tiny tables. A long bar, the first thing to greet customers as they entered, was along one wall. The pocket-sized bandstand protruded from the center of the opposite wall. For the musicians it was not just an intimate setting—it could be almost claustrophobic at times. It was called the Blackhawk and it was to become the congenial home for Dave Brubeck, the Trio, the Octet, and later the Quartet for more than six years.

Cacianti and his partners, Helen and Johnny Noga, had bought the place the year before and had changed its name from the Stork Club to the Blackhawk, perhaps inspired in the choice by memories of the Chicago room where, more than a decade before, the Bob Crosby band had gotten its first taste of glory, bringing Dixieland into Swing. The club began with mostly comedy acts.

The name of the club caused for an odd, unexpected controversy that arose when the publisher of this book sent the manuscript out for opinions from independent, expert reviewers. One of these readers insisted that "Blackhawk" should be spelled "Black Hawk," and offered as proof an old photograph of the club's marquee. The photo shows (below a billing for Miles Davis) a slight separation between the first *K* and the *H,* with a cocktail glass in the center. The picture appeared in a Columbia album, *Miles Davis in Person at the Blackhawk* (note spelling). All through the album's liner notes, and in liner notes on all Columbia albums with Dave Brubeck, the club's name is a single word. Dave and Iola remember it that way (although Iola was taken aback by the aforementioned photo). And jazz historian, writer and longtime Brubeck friend, Grover Sales, is sure it was "Black Hawk." Also, some of the early Fantasy releases used the two-word spelling.

The conflict was resolved in talking with the club's original owners. Both John Noga, living now in Los Angeles, and Guido Cacianti, who resides in Valley Springs in California's gold country, laughed, laughed some more, and then said, "It was *one* word!" How about the sign in front of the club? "Who knows?" said Noga; "It doesn't make any difference. It's one word." And Cacianti commented, "The guy who made the sign goofed. That's just the way he made it."

At the time the Nogas and Guido Cacianti bought what was soon to be renamed the Blackhawk, San Francisco was bursting with great entertainment—comedy, song, jazz of every kind—and with clubs like Bop City and the Say When, where still-emerging bop was dominant, and the Hangover, long home to Earl Hines and Joe Sullivan. Soon the hungry i, the Purple Onion, and many other showrooms were booking folk singers and outrageous, irreverent monologuists and comedians such as Lenny Bruce, Mort Sahl, and Phyllis Diller. At the time, Dave was virtually oblivious to this side of the entertainment world, but a few years later he met Bruce when both were working the Crescendo, Gene Norman's famous club on Sunset Boulevard in Hollywood. They immediately became friends, and Bruce later became close to the oldest Brubeck son, Darius. Dave remembers that Bruce and Darius used to hang out around the pool at the Chateau Marmount—Bruce acting as sort of a baby sitter.

Meanwhile, Paul Desmond had met comedian Mort Sahl and brought him to hear Lenny Bruce, by then performing at a club in the San Fernando Valley. Paul also brought Mort to hear the Quartet; that's how Dave and Mort first met. By the end of the summer of 1954, they were close enough so that Sahl and Desmond in one car and Dave and Iola in another caravaned north to San Francisco, stopping in Carmel for the Quartet to play a concert at the Sunset Auditorium. At the suggestion of Desmond, Mort did a stand-up turn during intermission—his first non-nightclub appearance. The event was taped and released several years later on Fantasy (*Mort Sahl at Sunset,* Fantasy No. 7005) as an early testament to a man who could improvise with words as well as any jazz artist could with music. Dave, Lenny (to the end of his short life), and Mort remained friends, although they weren't associated as professionals.

Back in 1949, the Brubecks had more dreams for the future than money for the present. Postwar euphoria enveloped the whole nation, not just California. Coast-to-coast, all things seemed possible. The United States auto industry produced a record six million cars, and General Motors reported profits of five hundred million dollars in just three quarters. *South Pacific* opened; *Death of a Salesman* won the Pulitzer Prize; the first Emmy awards were given. Dark clouds over Korea were as yet unnoticed. California was undergoing its second gold rush, with hundreds of thousands of veterans, many having visited the promised land during World War II, joining restless immigrants from all over the country in a mass migration to the gentle weather and the promise of unlimited opportunity.

Dave Brubeck and his family were "locals," of course: rare native Californians. More than that, it was life in San Francisco they loved. Dave says, "You know, if the Blackhawk would have hired us year-round, I'd never have left San Francisco. I really never wanted to leave, and I was satisfied with working for scale." Just over scale is what the Trio was paid at the Blackhawk originally, something under six hundred dollars a week to be divided between three musicians, for six nights and Sunday afternoon. There were five shows a night as Dave's guys alternated with a second group (later led by Cal Tjader for many years) from about 9:00 P.M. to two o'clock the next morning.

Once again it was Jimmy Lyons who providentially intervened, talking Guido into hiring Brubeck. The Trio had been working across the Bay at the Burma Lounge in Oakland (a gig also inspired by Lyons) and playing casuals in the area. At the Blackhawk, the change from the "square acts" to contemporary jazz didn't attract mobs of customers overnight, but before long the Trio, with Cal Tjader on drums and sometimes vibes and Ron Crotty on bass, began to attract the attention of college kids and other musicians. There was a door charge of one dollar per person and a minimum of two drinks per customer priced at a dollar and a quarter. The serious drinkers didn't come; the audience, from the beginning, was respectful of the musicians: they were there to listen. Brubeck's group worked six months out of the year at the Blackhawk, all during the months when the colleges and universities were in session, and they'd be replaced in the summer by other groups such as Vince Guaraldi's and Cal Tjader's and various visiting jazz stars from Los Angeles and the East Coast.

Sunday afternoons at the Blackhawk, the Octet—usually with Dave Van Kriedt on tenor sax, Paul Desmond on alto, Bill Smith on clarinet, Dick Collins on trumpet, Bob Collins on trombone, Jack Weeks on bass, and Tjader on drums—played a session all winter and spring. The personnel would change slightly from time-to-time as conflicting gigs dictated. Bay area teenagers, perhaps sparked by word from their college-age siblings, developed an extraordinary interest in the Octet. So the Nogas and Guido Cacianti set up a special section of the club for kids (Cacianti referred to them as "teen agents"). The teen section was separated from the rest of the jam-packed room by a barrier. "The best way I could describe it was to call it a cyclone fence," says Brubeck. "It was between the kids and their parents and the regular audience. There was no way the kids could get to the bar or mix with the drinking customers. There was a big uproar in the *Chronicle* and at city hall about it. Even the mayor got into it!" The owners prevailed, however, and thus a whole generation of jazz fans was nurtured.

Brubeck found the ambiance at the Sunday afternoon sessions ideal. Total attention was given to the music and musicians. That happened in the final set on most nights, too, as other musicians from visiting big bands and the hotels would drop in, and celebrities such as Ella Fitzgerald would come to both listen and sit in. Duke Ellington, George Shearing, Charlie Parker, Charles Mingus, and countless others became regulars when in town and spread the fame of both the club and its young stars. When summer came, Dave would go on tour to make a necessary buck, although he hated to be away from Iola and the growing family.

In 1951, the Trio, with Jack Weeks replacing Ron Crotty on bass (while Crotty did his military time), was booked into the Zebra Room in Honolulu. There the Trio came to an end and so, very nearly, did Dave Brubeck.

Dave, who had his family with him this time, had rented a small apartment near Waikiki. One fateful afternoon he took the kids bodysurfing.

Dave told the story this way during an informal 1992 interview in his workshop at his home in Wilton, Connecticut: "I said, 'Watch Daddy,' and I was going to dive into this wave and skim down the beach. The wave just disappeared on me, and there was a sand bar. Rather than hit head-on, as I should have done, I turned my neck, which dislocated and crushed vertebrae. The lifeguard and some Hawaiian beach buddies got me out of there to a nearby doctor, who sent me on to a hospital, which wouldn't accept me because I had no money. That hospital sent me on to Tripler veterans' hospital. Tripler sent an ambulance for me. On my way to the hospital I heard them say DOA. I was fading in and out of consciousness. The doctors finally called Iola about midnight because she had stayed behind with Darius and Michael. For about eight hours, she didn't even know where I was. They said to her, 'You can relax a little because we don't think he's going to be paralyzed.' It was months before I could play again. I still hurt every day of my life."

So severe was the lasting damage that, at the end of performances after he returned to work, the stage would have to "go to black" at the end of a set so that Dave could slowly pull himself up and stand there in the dark until he could get his legs to work to walk off the stage. For years, Dave stood up most of the way on cross-country flights; driving, he says, turns him into a basket case. He composes standing up, with a tall easel and a keyboard above it. He has had to change his playing technique to accommodate nerve damage.

The recuperation was long. Cal and Jack returned to the mainland.

As Dave lay in traction at Tripler, considering his future, he learned that Cal and Jack had been met at the airport in San Francisco by Max and Sol Weiss, owners of Fantasy Records. At the time, Dave believed that he was an equal owner of Fantasy. Max and Sol had a proposal for the two members of the Dave Brubeck Trio. "They were told to find another piano player and start their own group," recalls Dave with sadness. He adds, "I objected to this, saying that I feel like I'm the one who contributed artistically to Fantasy the most. I think you should wait until I get well before you take two-thirds of my group and put them with another piano player! Wait till I get well. So they started a new label, Galaxy [the name, like Fantasy, taken from a science-fiction magazine], and put the Cal Tjader Trio on that!" This maneuver did not speed Dave's recovery.

The idea for a new quartet was born in the pain of recovering from both the surfing injuries and the loss of Cal and Jack. Although it was a blow at first, having to form a new group began to appeal to Dave's innate interest in experimenting. Then too, he had worked so well musically with Paul Desmond, albeit haphazardly career-wise, that adding Paul's horn seemed natural. A third motivation was the knowledge that carrying the solo improvisation role for an entire night's gig with only a rhythm section to back him up would be much more taxing in his physical condition and might even result in relapse. Paul Desmond's sax work would share that load easily and, Dave knew, beneficially as well.

So Dave wrote (with pencil and paper over his head) to old friend Paul Desmond and asked him to get a rhythm section together so that a quartet could be formed when Dave was able to work again. Dave left the personnel selection to Paul, telling him only whom he *didn't* want. He doesn't remember, for sure, who the initial drummer was that Paul had picked, but the bassist was Wyatt "Bull" Ruther, followed by Fred Dutton, who later became first bassoonist with the Los Angeles Philharmonic. Dutton's bassoon can be heard on Fantasy Records with the quartet in "Crazy Chris" and "A Foggy Day."

The Quartet—but not yet the Classic Dave Brubeck Quartet—opened to a very warm reception at the Blackhawk for most of the winter season and made the initial records for Fantasy. Although this group gradually found a following even wider than the trio's, keeping Desmond in his chair wasn't easy. "He did some rather immature things," says Dave. "He said we were getting stale playing the same things every night, that we should take a vacation. He said he wanted to go back up to the Feather River." Memories of earlier incidents were enough to telegraph a warning to Dave, but the group acceded to Desmond's request and signed off temporarily. "But then," continues Dave, "Paul stayed at the Blackhawk as an intermission pianist. He told me a complete phony story. I didn't know anything about it until Guido called me and said, 'Paul isn't doing so well as a solo pianist. When are you guys gonna come back in?'"

Desmond left the group, which returned to a trio status. Shortly thereafter, Dave was walking down Market Street and ran into Paul's father, who stopped Dave and urged him to take Paul back in yet once more. "He said, 'You've got to do it,' and I said, 'Why? He'll do fine on his own.' And he said, 'You don't know Paul like I do. He's got to have you as a leader, to guide him.'" And Paul did return shortly thereafter, again with no apologies and no explanations for his defection.

Audiences became ever bigger, and the Quartet began getting awards, including the first Black jazz poll, conducted by the *Pittsburgh Courier,* one of the nation's leading Black newspapers. No other White group was even mentioned. "We were number one. All the rest were Black," says Dave. In fact, he recalls, the Quartet had such a Black following that, in the six months off from the Blackhawk every year, they'd sometimes work many Black clubs across the South. When they played in these communities, where White people seldom came, they'd be mobbed by fans.

"We were playing in the Walahage Hotel that catered to the Black clientele in Atlanta," Dave adds. "The owner had four sons: 'Wa' was Walter, 'La' was Lawrence. 'Ha' was Harold. 'Ge' was George. *Wa-la-ha-ge Hotel!* Everybody thought it was an African name. Performers had suites at the hotel, but we weren't allowed to stay in them because Atlanta was still segregated.

"Clubs like that used to put ropes down the middle with Whites on one side, Blacks on the other. By the time the night was over, that rope had been climbed many times from both directions. The owner would say, 'Well, folks, I do have the rope there, and you're supposed to stay on your side,' just to obey the law. I had lots of laughs about integration. Some situations were so ridiculous I couldn't tell you. But they'll never leave my mind because we'd get treated sometimes, in *that* part of town, as Blacks would be treated in the *other* part of town. You had to have a sense of humor. I think that's why Blacks have been able to tolerate such injustice. It's either that or you go crazy."

Remembering that Dave was always a deeply committed family man, it's easy to understand why those off-season road trips were so painful for him. With that in mind, Iola one day came up with an entirely new concept that quite incidentally revolutionized the old one-nighter, road-trip concept. She searched the list of colleges and universities in the *World Almanac* for every institution on the West Coast, and personally wrote to more than one hundred of them, suggesting the Brubeck Quartet as great entertainment for campus concerts, citing their recordings and reviews. So successful did these events become that they spread nationwide and opened an entirely new avenue for expression and income for jazz groups everywhere. Before that, many bands had played college dances and fraternity parties, but very few concerts.

For Dave, there was an important side benefit to the campus gigs. Often, the school's radio station would ask permission to tape a concert for one on-campus broadcast of the program. Dave would say, "Yes, but I want the tapes after that broadcast." He began to build a library of exciting, live performances. *Jazz at College of the Pacific* and *Jazz at Oberlin* (both on the Fantasy label) attest to the joyous interplay at these sessions. They also display, generally, a somewhat less percussive and less adventurous Brubeck than the later one on Columbia records.

Brubeck had first recorded professionally in a modest and experimental way in 1949. The Trio had become solidly established at the Burma Lounge in Oakland, and Jimmy Lyons had arranged for the group to be broadcast live, once a week, over KNBC in San Francisco. All this local attention led to a session at Sound Recorders in San Francisco where the fledgling Ampex Company had delivered some prototype tape equipment. This was a session for Coronet Records, owned by Dixieland trombonist Jack Sheedy. San Francisco was

Dixie-crazy at the time, what with Lu Watters and his Yerba Buena Jazz Band and other traditionalists, but Sheedy was not finding the recording business a profitable one for him and took a chance on a new brand of jazz. Acting as recording engineer was Sol Weiss, who, with his brother Max, owned Circle Records, the local pressing plant that actually stamped Coronet's end product.

Dave, bassist Ron Crotty, and drummer Cal Tjader showed up early, and the session, tape decks rolling uncertainly, got under way as scheduled. "We could never get the Ampex machine up to speed," Dave remembers, "and we were two and a half hours in on a three-hour session, so they went back to acetate. Our first recordings to actually be released had to be made one after another in the remaining half-hour. Three of them were done in one take, and the other in two takes. That's the way we had to start. There was no editing. And they're still selling those records."

The sides the Trio managed to complete in that historic half-hour were "Blue Moon," "Tea for Two," "Laura," and "Indiana." "Blue Moon" was chosen "Record of the Month," commended as a "poly-tonal experiment," by *Metronome*. "Indiana" turns up (digitally remastered) as the second track in Columbia's four-CD Brubeck collection, *Time Signatures*. It begins as a quite romantic statement and modulates to a steamy tempo by way of a Mozart-like riff, to which it returns two minutes and thirty seconds later (fitting nicely onto a 78 rpm side). Dave's piano style had already matured and was very clearly his own. Nobody could mistake him for another player. The recording itself has remarkably good fidelity and balance.

Sheedy, however, found he couldn't pay his bills, and so the Weiss brothers and Dave bought back the masters for what Dave remembers as "about three hundred dollars." Together they started the Fantasy label.

Fantasy eventually became an industry giant. The Brubecks, however, didn't share in the profits when the Weiss brothers sold out to Sol Zaentz in the mid-1960s (who in turn bought a number of other important labels). Discussion of the Fantasy sale is still painful to Dave and Iola, but in early 1995 Dave told the story as best he could remember. "In the contract I had with the Weiss brothers, I agreed to pay the musicians on recording dates and they'd pay the technical costs of making the records and the pressings and that sort of thing.

But the sole ownership of the name "Fantasy" remained in Sol Weiss's name. At the time I signed, I didn't understand that that clause kept me from being a true partner. We put everything into that company, including bringing in a lot of other talent. When we learned that our only equity was in my own records, it was a real shock."

Iola remembers the event in this way: "I don't remember the exact year, but I know we were living on the campus at Mills College and, one Friday or Saturday, Sol and maybe Max came around and talked to Dave about the future of the company and working out how many albums Dave would record for the company and that sort of thing. Then the Weisses went to Los Angeles, and when they came back on Monday or Tuesday, they called Dave and said basically that Dave had nothing to do with the company anymore! They wanted him to continue to record, but a partner he was not. We can only guess at what happened over the weekend or what kind of advice they got or from whom."

Looking back, Dave and Iola could see a clue as to what finally occurred in the 1951 incident, while Dave was recuperating from his diving accident, when Cal Tjader and Jack Weeks had been told to "find another piano player." But Dave points out emphatically that he and Cal remained friends until Cal died, and that he and Jack Weeks continue to remain friends. As for the Weiss brothers, Dave says, "I always try to keep a good feeling, and when I went to Columbia, it was understood that I'd still record one album a year for Fantasy, so it wasn't a complete break. At first I thought, 'There goes all my work for nothing,' and then, when I signed with Columbia, I could see that fate had guided me in a direction I didn't want to go and it was a very good direction. If the break hadn't happened with Fantasy, I'd never have gone with Columbia. And, if I hadn't done the recording with Fantasy, I wouldn't have gotten all that national exposure."

However, to resume the story about the early Fantasy days, after the first Trio sides there was another Trio session. Dave wanted to record the Octet, but that could not be done until the initial Fantasy investment was recovered. Each session had to subsidize the next. Dave, acting as artist and repertoire (A & R) man, got the Red Norvo Trio with Charles Mingus and guitarist Tal Farlow and the Gerry Mulligan Quartet with trumpeter Chet Baker to record for the little company. The *Dave Brubeck Discography* by Dr. Klaus-Gotthard Fischer lists fifteen twelve-inch LP releases and twenty-nine single 78s (two selections on each) on Fantasy. These recordings have been reissued countless times in different combinations and formats.

The Octet was finally recorded by Fantasy. It had the old nucleus of Milhaud students: Dave Van Kriedt on tenor; Bill Smith, clarinet; Dick Collins, trumpet; Jack Weeks on bass; and Dave at the piano. Dick Collins' brother, Bob, was added on trombone and Paul Desmond, the perennial "sitter-in" of that period, played alto. Cal Tjader was usually the drummer. Although earlier tapes from concerts and NBC programs were later released, the first real recording session, which included "The Way You Look Tonight," occurred in 1950. Dave says, "The session was lavish in the use of counterpoint and polyrhythms, with a Picasso-style portrait of the Octet by Original Basil Johns on the cover [of the album]. He was one of the most enthusiastic of our friends and supporters."

Listening to the Octet today brings back echoes of what became known as West Coast Jazz: cool and intellectual, not particularly swinging. It got interesting reviews but was too radical and cerebral for real popular success. The Trio was the bread and butter for Fantasy and club engagements until the Quartet was organized after Dave's near-fatal diving accident in Hawaii in 1951.

The Quartet, with Wyatt "Bull" Ruther on bass, Herb Barman on drums and Dave and Paul as the solo voices first turns up in a Fantasy release taken from a 1951 NBC broadcast at the Surf Club in Hollywood. It *does* swing. So does the group that performed (and was recorded) at Oberlin College, the renowned conservatory in Ohio, on March 2, 1953. On "Perdido," listen to Dave's "locked hands" solo and Paul's totally exuberant first solo and the chase choruses at the end, and you can see why the classically-trained students recognized this as great music and responded appropriately. Both Paul and Dave always considered this one of the very best of their recorded performances. Lloyd Davis was on drums and Ron Crotty had returned as bassist. Says Dave, "Paul and I seemed to have some kind of telepathic communication. We could anticipate each other's thoughts to the uncanny extent we would even make the same mistake together and then correct it, in the same way, together. We seemed able to spin out our contrapuntal lines anticipating each other's thoughts. If any two musicians were destined to play together, it was Desmond and I."

Dave had the Quartet recorded at the College of the Pacific, at Storyville in Boston, at the Wilshire Ebell in Los Angeles. Fantasy also recorded sometimes, without notice or permission, at San Francisco's Blackhawk. Dave says they had mikes hung in the air circulating ducts. Some of these takes didn't meet with approval by Brubeck but, in those rough-and-tumble formative years, he'd have no veto. He does say the group was always paid, if only scale. Of course, there was no money from the countless "bootleg" recordings taken off the air or (in later years) made by customers with hidden tape recorders.

A key producer at then CBS-owned Columbia Records, George Avakian, came to the Bay area in the summer of 1954 to be with his wife, the violinist Anahid Ajemian, who was doing a series of concerts with her sister Maro on KQED radio. Avakian took advantage of the opportunity to listen to some local talent. He did this at a time when industry executives rarely sought out new artists anywhere but in New York City. Avakian went to the Blackhawk. He was aware of the music polls the Brubeck group was winning and had heard some of the Fantasy records. "The impact, in person, of the Quartet was quite different from what I had expected," says Avakian. "It wasn't as aggressive as, for instance, Art Blakey's Jazz Messengers, but depended on a rhythmic excitement that was understated and more relaxed. There was a wonderful contrast between Dave, who was an explosive player in up-tempo pieces, and Paul, who was laid-back and 'floating.' It was a combination of styles that don't sound as though they would fit together, yet we all know they did. The impact of seeing the group together for the first time completely sold me. I decided, then and there, that I had to sign the Dave Brubeck Quartet."

Dave, at the time coming to an end of a three-year contract with Fantasy, liked the idea, too. Concrete negotiations came a little later, and when Avakian asked Brubeck what he wanted in the contract, Dave said, "I'd like to have a guarantee of six thousand dollars because that would allow me to start building a home." Avakian responded, "Well, Dave, I hope we make the money back in a reasonable length of time."

Part of the deal was the collection of campus concerts Dave had stored away. Columbia's first issue was *Jazz Goes to College,* released June 6, 1955. On June 30, Columbia President Jim Conklin called George Avakian to say that the six-thousand-dollar advance was already exceeded and that Dave was due to get an additional check. Oberlin College and the University of Michigan were the settings for these tapes, made by campus radio stations and painstakingly enhanced by George Avakian and Columbia's best engineers. *Jazz at Storyville* followed, taken from a live appearance at Boston's club of that name.

It should be noted that both Columbia and Fantasy released many of these Brubeck-owned tapes at different times and with different mixes of titles. The Columbia issues, having been re-equalized and otherwise doctored by top audio engineers, are far kinder to the ear, but the Fantasy disks contain some excellent material not on Columbia.

The symbiotic relationship between the recording industry and musicians and singers is complicated. It has been so since the days of the Edison cylinder, through the long era of the 78s, the short reign of the 45s, and the triumph of the LPs. It continues with CDs and will surely haunt whatever comes next, probably some form of digital recording involving chips and no troublesome moving parts.

Chaos has characterized much of the history of the industry. Changes in ownership have been the rule, especially during the depression when Victor was forced to sell out to RCA and Columbia to CBS. Those were the two dominant labels; they had few serious challengers, excepting the Kapp Brothers' Decca Records. The Brunswick label had, for years, been a serious player in the market with a substantial roster that included Teddy Wilson, Billie Holiday, Red Norvo, and Duke Ellington. But it, too, became a depression casualty, selling out to Columbia, as did Epic, Okeh, and Vocalion. There were, of course, many much smaller companies, specializing in jazz, folk, and what were euphemistically called "race records" (produced for the Black consumer). Among these, Commodore, Vanguard, and Blue Note come to mind.

In the early forties, songwriter-singer Johnny Mercer with another songwriter and producer Buddy DeSylva and record store owner Glenn Wallich started Capitol Records—a rare example of a recording company owned and run by those who were musically talented and to whom business success came as a result of that musicality combined with inspiration and good taste. Today Capitol is owned by the British EMI, RCA Victor by a European consortium, Columbia by Sony, and Decca by MCA, which was purchased by Japan's Matsusita, a multinational giant. In turn, Matsusita sold control to Canada's Seagram in 1995. The historic Decca masters were a very small part of all this wheeling and dealing.

It's easy to see why the money guys have made most of the final decisions on whom to sign, what to record, and how to promote. It's an unhappy fact, also, that many, many artists have been shortchanged and sometimes deliberately swindled out of precious royalties. Yet it is undeniable that the record companies exist on talent, and talent desperately needs the exposure that recordings supply.

Radio broadcasting is a third element, one that has been sometimes uneasy and corrupt (remembering the days of flagrant payola). Still, it would be virtually impossible to find a major artist who has made it without a string of successful, well-promoted, and nationally distributed and broadcast records. Certainly Dave Brubeck has been no exception.

Brubeck, however, during the major years of his long career, has had the great good luck to be associated with responsible executives and talented, genuinely musical, willing-to-take-a-chance artist-and-repertoire people. Dave has also, most of the way, had very good legal advice and, since Russell Gloyd joined the team in the late seventies as personal manager and producer, has had solid support, both personal and professional. All this comes in handy when it comes to contract signing and enforcement.

Time for the Big Time

On November 8, 1954, five years after the debut of the Quartet at the Blackhawk, Dave Brubeck was selected as the cover story subject for *Time* magazine, with a striking Boris Artzybasheff painting as the cover art.

Time had, a little earlier, sent reporter Carter Harman to cover the Quartet's first studio recording for Columbia, *Brubeck Time*. The acoustically glorious Thirtieth Street studio also served as a movie set, for Gjon Mili was there to shoot the short film, *Jazz in the Movies*. George Avakian's brother, Aram, had persuaded Mili to film the Dave Brubeck Quartet, against Mili's protestations. Brubeck was understandably nervous, and after the first take, Mili said loudly, "My first impression was right. You're no damn good!"

That made Dave's blood boil, and he became determined to prove Mili dead wrong. The Quartet jumped into an original called "Stompin' for Mili" in what Dave remembers as a musical expression of rage and frustration. "We ended with the feeling we had redeemed ourselves. I can still see Mili jumping from his chair exclaiming, 'You're hot! By God, you're hot! Don't stop now!'" *Time* magazine used that as a choice quote in its piece on Dave.

Scheduled next was a minor blues. Brubeck remembers that Mili said, "I would like (closing his eyes and raising his hand expressively) to see Audrey Hepburn walking through the woods."

"Gee," said Paul Desmond, "so would I."

"One," Brubeck said, noticing the glazed expression in Paul's eyes, "two, three, four." And they played what became "Audrey." Paul was superb. Then, track-after-track, Dave, Paul, Joe Dodge on drums, and Bob Bates on bass made memorable music.

Columbia chose the *Time* cover as the centerpiece for the album cover, and *Brubeck Time* sold about one hundred thousand copies, about ten times as many as the most successful jazz albums sold in those days.

It happened again with *Jazz Goes to Junior College* made up of tracks from campus recordings, owned by Dave, that had been done earlier at Fullerton and Long Beach Junior Colleges in California. The album was released on June 6, 1955. Critical comment was warm, and public response ever more encouraging.

After all the publicity generated by *Time* magazine, *Jazz: Red, Hot and Cool,* recorded live at Basin Street East, had a merchandising tie-in with Helena Rubenstein, that firm having produced a new line of "Red, Hot and Cool" cosmetics. The cross-plugging didn't hurt, and that album, too, was a big seller. "The Duke," one of Brubeck's most successful compositions, later to be performed by countless other artists, made its first appearance in this album. In his liner notes for Columbia's boxed set *Time Signatures,* Dave recalled, "The idea for 'The Duke' came to me when I was in the car, taking my son Chris to nursery school. The original title was 'The Duke Meets Darius Milhaud.' When I first wrote it, I didn't really understand how complex it was. It goes through all twelve keys in its first eight bars. It hits all the roots. It could be the first jazz tune that does that."

Edward Kennedy Ellington had long been a Brubeck fan (the feeling was reciprocal) and had even heard Dave with The Three D's in San Francisco's Geary Cellar. To many listeners, the Ellington feel in "The Duke" was immediately apparent, but Brubeck says, "One of the better-known critics wrote about that piece that it 'had nothing to do with Ellington.' I know he knows Ellington, but he doesn't know the Ellington *I* know, because recently I heard what must have influenced me in 'The Duke,' and it was very similar to something the Duke had done very early, the title of which I wish I could remember. I do find a little of 'Jack the Bear' in 'The Duke.'" The real-life Jack the Bear was a Harlem bass player, and Ellington's composition was written to star bassist Jimmy Blanton. It combined a *ritornello*, a thirty-two-bar song form, with five choruses of twelve-bar blues. Years after Blanton's death, Brubeck came to know a successor Alvin "Junior" Raglin, who still played Blanton's set-piece. It was Raglin whom Dave ran into backstage at an Ellington one-nighter in California. This was in the early 1940s, and Dave was still a student. Responding to Dave's wish to meet the celebrated composer-leader-pianist, Raglin led Brubeck to Ellington's dressing room. Dave walked in and was so awed he couldn't say a word.

An interesting postscript to the affection between Ellington and Brubeck lies in something Dave says the Duke, shortly before he died, told his son, Mercer, "I don't want people to think I had only Black friends. This year I want Louie Bellson and Dave Brubeck appointed Ellington Fellows at Yale."

As Dave says, "Kinship doesn't come from skin color. It's your soul and your mind."

In April 1956, the Brubecks were living in their dream home in the Oakland Hills high above the Bay. Dave had purchased one of the then-state-of-the-art Ampex tape recorders and producer George Avakian, back in New York, sent some reels of used tape about to be tossed by Columbia. Dave began to record himself, solo piano (generally late at night, after the kids were asleep). He'd then send samples back to Avakian. Eventually, says George, "This resulted in *Brubeck Plays Brubeck,* which included the first recording of 'Two Part Contention' (a play on 'two part invention') as well as solo treatments of 'The Duke' and 'In Your Own Sweet Way.'" It's interesting to note that the next Brubeck solo album wasn't recorded until 1994 for Telarc's release entitled *Just You, Just Me.*

It's not surprising that Dave Brubeck has always preferred live recordings over studio sessions. From *Jazz Goes to College* in 1954 to *Moscow Night* in 1987 (Concord Jazz) to *Late Night Brubeck,* recorded live at the Blue Note in New York City by Telarc in the fall of 1993—this preference has shown that spontaneous inventions can be lifted to new heights by audience reaction. There is nothing like the total magic of loving and being loved that a large, live, joyous audience can provide. It makes no difference where you are or what language is spoken, for the language of music is universal. Dave often referred to the audience as the "fifth member of the Quartet."

In the fall of 1956, drummer Joe Morello replaced Joe Dodge, who wanted to get home and off the road. At the end of 1957, Eugene Wright entered on bass, taking over from Norman Bates, who had also had enough of the road and was anxious to stay with his wife and children in San Francisco. Wright, Morello, Desmond, and Brubeck became, then, the Classic Quartet.

Fatigue, illness, worries about families, bad weather—none of these things seem to have affected the Classic Quartet if the audience was ready to be entertained and to be a part of the show. A prime example was the Carnegie Hall concert of February 21, 1963, which resulted in two Columbia albums and which all members of the Quartet consider just about the best of all their concert performances.

Says Joe Morello, "We had just flown into JFK and went directly to the hall. I had this cold, and I had a fever. I was sweating profusely, and I didn't want to play. Nobody wanted to play. All kinds of friends kept coming backstage to see me, and I kept saying, 'Man, I just don't want to go out there.' But as soon as we started playing, it was electrifying. The audience was so with us that everything went down right. It was perfect. There was not one splice in that album."

Brubeck, remembering that same concert, says, "Everyone was taking unbelievable risks. Joe Morello was in one or two time signatures; Eugene Wright was in another. Paul and I were free in another one, and it was just *working* all night. I felt so good because the band was doing what I wanted it to do rhythmically, but one of the big critics said, 'They couldn't even keep time together.' That critic wasn't ready for the concept of multiple time. His feet, his ears, his body wasn't ready. But Mingus was ready, and Parker was ready, and the Duke was ready. Duke once commented at one of my concerts, 'That's what jazz is all about.' Most important, the *audience* was ready that night at Carnegie."

The wild, experimental nature of the evening didn't involve just multiple time. Dave told author and critic George Simon, who wrote the liner notes for the albums, about what happened during the very first number, "St. Louis Blues," which Dave has almost always used as the opener. "I'm playing in E major with my left hand and G major with my right. Now, I've been on a polytonal kick for twenty years, but I've never in my life improvised with this particular key relationship before." Later, Dave found himself moving from one key to another, against home key G major.

According to the Klaus-Gotthard Fischer discography, which Dave and Iola believe is the most definitive, Dave and the Quartet did fifty albums for Columbia. He had been signed to do three a year but often did more, and as pleasing as the live recordings were, the studio sessions offered clear advantages. One was the opportunity to do concept albums like *Jazz Impressions of the USA, Jazz Impressions of Eurasia, Time Out, Time Further Out, Time in Outer Space,* and *Time In.*

"Things were planned in advance, and you'd just go in and go to work. Usually, everybody played their best because they knew it would be there forever." Usually, after a take on one number, everybody would go back into the control room and listen to a playback. "Each guy is listening to himself," says Dave. "And then I'd say, 'Come on. Let's listen one more time to see how the *group* thing is.'" If Joe, Paul, Gene, or Dave didn't like something about their own performance, there'd immediately be another take. Sometimes there'd be a take that maybe Dave didn't like as well as another but in which another Quartet member had a particularly exciting solo and that would be the one OK'd for release. Yet more rarely, several takes were spliced together to create something as close as possible to overall perfection. More often than not, the very first take turned out to be the best. Never, according to Brubeck, was a whole session aborted because it wasn't going well. The making of albums was just something this wonderfully cohesive group could do without pain or strain. Dave remembers that Paul Desmond used to say, "We could make an album for a streetcar token and a ham sandwich."

The parade of twelve-inch Columbia albums continued. There were *Dave Brubeck and Jay and Kai in Newport, Dave Digs Disney* (from which came the classic "Someday My Prince Will Come"), *Newport 1958* (recorded under impossible weather conditions), *The*

Dave Brubeck Quartet in Europe, and *Gone with the Wind.* This last may have been the most swinging and melodically delightful of the Quartet albums so far. Its distinction was due in part to the choice of material. Each player included a personal favorite. It was "Ol' Man River" for Eugene Wright, "Short'nin' Bread" for Joe Morello, "Basin Street" and "Lonesome Road" for Paul, and "Georgia on My Mind" and "Swanee River" for Dave. Some of the tracks were played by the group *as* a group for the first time in the studio. It was first take almost all the way.

In the entire history of the Classic Brubeck Quartet, the most important recording session was that of July 1, 1959.

Dozens of singles had been released by Fantasy and Columbia, both in 78 rpm and, later, in 45 rpm formats, but Dave had never had a hit. A hit, in fact, was an unheard-of concept for a contemporary jazz group. *Time Out* produced "Take Five," and "Take Five" took off like the Boeing 707, which made its commercial debut that year. Each selection in the album had a different time signature. It was 5/4 for "Take Five." Dave says, "We credit Paul Desmond as composer. But I know the whole story, and *I'd* have to credit Joe Morello with coming up with that beat. I used to say to Paul, 'Why don't you put a melody to this rhythm Joe is playing?' So they'd mess around backstage. And I'd say, 'Now *write* something, Paul, that goes with it.' So he came in with some themes, but he didn't have a completed composition. I put two of Paul's themes together, so we gave the composition credit to him. But when people want to know the full story, they should talk to Joe. Because Joe said 'Take Five' was basically his 5/4 beat. And I have to agree with him."

According to Morello, it all stemmed from his being bored with 4/4 during his solos. He says he started doing 5/4 just for fun. "Even after 'Take Five' was recorded," Joe says, "nobody expected it to be successful. It was written just to close a show with a drum solo. That's all it was. It was a good vehicle for me because I was very comfortable in that time signature." Now, of course, Dave can't do a concert without including that piece.

"Blue Rondo a la Turk" also came from the *Time Out* album. "It is the blues, it is a rondo, exact rondo form, it was written in Turkey, and it's a play on Mozart's 'Rondo a la Turk,'" says Dave, explaining the genesis of this adventure in 9/8 time. "That's one-two, one-two, one-two, one-two-three," Dave counts. "I first heard the rhythm on the street in Istanbul on the way to the radio station, where I was to meet with the big radio orchestra. I stayed on the street corner, trying to get this rhythm down. I finally got it in my head and sang it all the way to the studio. I asked the orchestra, 'What is this rhythm: one-two, one-two, one-two, one-two-three?' I finished the first bar, and the entire orchestra started improvising in 9/8. I couldn't believe it. They said, 'It's like the blues to you, 9/8 is to us.'" Dave says there was a Turkish jazz musician with him that day whose name was June Eight. He was born on that date, and that's his name ("or they were putting me on!"). Virtually all jazz groups who tour Turkey get to know him. He told Dave that 9/8 was a very old Turkish rhythm. "Blue Rondo" starts and finishes in 9/8, but at the perfect moment it switches, as a release, into swinging 4/4. Even so, when Goddard Lieberson chose it to back "Take Five" for the single derived from the album, he had a major battle with Columbia's sales department. Lieberson, a very musical, very far-sighted man, was then president of the company, but neither track would have been released without great effort on his part. "It isn't in 4/4. Nobody can dance to it," said the sales department.

The next Brubeck release combined the Quartet, recorded in New York, and the Trio (Brubeck, Wright, and Morello), recorded in Los Angeles, both sessions in October of 1959. Here the music was very mainstream, perhaps in response to the brouhaha over *Time Out*. Even "Deep in the Heart of Texas" and "Jeannie with the Light Brown Hair" were included. The music was exciting but not particularly adventurous.

Adventurous, however, does apply to the following release, *The Riddle*. It stars the piece's composer, long-time Brubeck friend (and member of the original Octet) Bill Smith on clarinet, with the Morello-Wright rhythm section. The basic theme is the old folk song "Hey, Ho, Anybody Home." As Dave said in the liner notes, "The first riddle is to discover the thematic relationship of each of the tunes. The second riddle is to determine which parts of the music are written and which are improvised."

Next came a truly major recording project: *Bernstein Plays Brubeck Plays Bernstein*. Leonard Bernstein conducted the New York Philharmonic with the Dave Brubeck Quartet in a performance of *Dialogues for Jazz Combo and Orchestra,* composed by Dave's brother Howard. The Quartet alone also played selections from Bernstein's score for *West Side Story.* Bernstein was a friend of Howard. They had studied together at Tanglewood in Massachusetts. The piece was originally written by Howard for a performance with the San Diego Symphony. Dave says, "It was fortunate that Howard wanted to write a big piece. Bernstein heard about it, wanted to see the score, and liked it. Goddard Lieberson was all for it. Almost everything good that happened for me at Columbia happened when he was there."

Dialogues was just that: the orchestra strictly played the written score while the jazz combo was free to improvise on the material of the four movements: allegro, andante-ballad, adagio-ballad, and allegro-blues. After the initial rehearsal, the work was first performed at Carnegie Hall on December 10, 11, and 13, 1959. It was very well received by a rather sophisticated audience. On January 30, 1960, it was recorded.

About the recording session, Dave has this to say in the liner notes for Columbia's four-CD career retrospective. "Bernstein was great to work with, but also scary. The Quartet and the whole orchestra was sitting at Columbia's Thirtieth Street studios ten minutes after the session was supposed to start and there was no Bernstein. Naturally I was nervous because I was paying for half the session, and you know what it costs to record a symphony orchestra! Suddenly the door opens, and Bernstein comes in, goes straight to the podium as fast as he can walk, and says, 'Gentlemen, the session started with a ten minute break!'"

In February, the Quartet recorded with famed singer Jimmy Rushing. This was done at Rushing's request, and the dichotomy between blues-shouter and avant-garde combo was apparent, but swing won the day. There's a particularly delightful "Melancholy Baby" to hear. The Rushing recording sessions were completed in August 1960.

By now, you can see a pattern appear. Straight-ahead (or as straight as the Brubeck whims permit) jazz albums dominate but are punctuated by more daring off-beat projects. To define the intent of this chapter, only those albums that involve the Classic Quartet (Brubeck, Desmond, Morello, Wright) and the contexts in which it performed are covered in depth. Exceptions involve guest artists. Not all albums will be covered; there are too many.

The feast of new material began to appear at an accelerated rate. Some albums have proven more enduring and exciting than others. Let's look at some of the off-beat and often beguiling music that followed the first eighteen Columbia 12-inch LP releases.

Very rarely did Dave accompany singers in his recordings. When you consider all the remarkable vocalists under contract to Columbia at that time (Tony Bennett, Doris Day, Rosemary Clooney, Jo Stafford, Johnny Mathis, and many more), it's a particular tribute to Carmen McRae that she was chosen on three occasions.

First was a Brubeck-Brubeck-McRae project, in that Iola Brubeck wrote the lyrics to three of the nine tracks. Iola says, "I did not come from a musical background. I studied drama and English lit, and my attempt to write lyrics just came from living with this guy, and I do love those songs Carmen sang in the *Tonight Only!* album, especially 'Strange Meadowlark.' The melody is actually based on the meadowlark call, and I think that's what drew me to it first. Dave had already written the music when I added the lyrics."

The lyric reads:

What a strange meadowlark,
to be singing oh so sweetly in the park tonight.
All alone, meadowlark, are you dreaming of the moons that
burn so bright
and of love in flight?
Can't you sleep, meadowlark,
is there nothing left but whistling in the dark?
So sad.
Was it love, meadowlark?
Were the songs you sang last summer crazy mad?
Think of all you had.

The words suit the music: poignant, sweet, gentle. A similar mood continues in "Briar Bush." "Weep No More" has both words and music composed by Dave (and later revised by Iola) when he was still in the army. McRae's singing has an emotional impact that comes from understatement rather than heavy use of vocal trademarks. As Dave said, "Carmen has added even to my own understanding of the music."

Carmen joins Joe Morello for a tour de force for the drummer, "Paradiddle Joe," unheard since the days of Tony Pastor, whose Bluebird recording was a minor hit in 1941. Eugene Wright contributed "Talkin' and Walkin'" and shows how coherent a bass solo *can* be. Paul Desmond composed "Late Lament," a piece as melancholy as Dave's "Tristesse" in the same album. There's an extended blues, "Melanctha," on which both Desmond and Brubeck have space to stretch and swing.

McRae was also part of a much more ambitious undertaking. This was *The Real Ambassadors*. Iola describes it this way: "The idea was to incorporate some of the spirit, the emotion, and the wit of jazz into a Broadway show. Dave and I were seeking a reason for the jazz musicians to be onstage to tell their stories through their instruments as well as to sing and act." This was at a time when the Quartet had already toured the world, as had Louis Armstrong, Dizzy Gillespie, and others. Gillespie's was the first State Department–sponsored tour.

No Broadway performance of *The Real Ambassadors* was ever given. "It was done only once, and that was at the Monterey Jazz Festival (1962) with Iola on one stage, keeping the narrative going," says Dave, and Iola adds, "We had an all-star cast— Louis Armstrong and his group onstage with Dave Lambert, Jon Hendricks, and Yolanda Bavan and Carmen McRae. It was so wonderfully done and so enthusiastically embraced by the audience. The audience went absolutely nuts over it. For one thing, they saw Louis Armstrong in a different way than they had ever seen him before. There were jokes and songs, but while all that was going on, there was a very serious side, too. He was a good actor. He emoted in a real way that just touched everyone."

Dave makes the case for the production: "The whole idea was that Louis was the greatest ambassador that we had. We tried to take the racial situation and let Louis make people laugh at it. We had lines set up in it where we would show the ridiculousness of being segregated because of the color of your skin.

"It opens with the Bible. 'God created man in His image. In His image and likeness He created them.' Then, Lambert, Hendricks, and Ross (Annie Ross was on hand for the recording session in New York prior to the Monterey concert) are singing a Gregorian chant on those words, and Louis comes in singing the blues. 'They say I look like God. Could God be Black? My God! If both were made in the image of Thee, could Thou, perchance, a zebra be?'

"We thought the audience was going to laugh. We looked over and Louis had tears coming out of his eyes. There wasn't a laugh in the audience. All night Louie made 'em *think*. Even so, they wouldn't put it on Broadway. It would have been the forerunner of so much that happened. It was before *Raisin in the Sun* and some of the other plays that came along later. Producers were interested in it but afraid of it. Such a shame."

Iola Brubeck describes the Monterey performance as "one of the big events of our lives." She wrote the book and lyrics for *The Real Ambassadors*, and Dave composed the score. The show gave Dave a chance to record with one of his boyhood idols, pianist Billy Kyle. They are heard together on "Summer Song," "Cultural Exchange," and "Since Love Had Its Way." Carmen McRae sings "In the Lurch," "One Moment Worth Years," "I Didn't Know 'til You Told Me," and "Easy as You Go." It's often been noted that Dave wrote not only good tunes but came up with expressive titles for them.

"Unsquare Dance" was the Brubeck standard that came out of the June 8, 1961, session that produced the album *Time Further Out*. This was composed in 7/4 time. Dave says he never wrote down the tune; it came to him in the car as he was riding to the session. Nobody was more surprised than Dave that it became an international hit. "In Russia the people started clapping with it in perfect time," he says. "In Vienna, the whole audience erupted. Big surprise! This, by then, was an old tune you thought was dead and all of a sudden you play it, just because you want to play something different in a concert, and the whole place explodes. It's regional, and sometimes you figure out why. In Vienna, 'Unsquare Dance' is the theme song, the opening song, for a very popular TV show, and it's also on TV now in England. Every time there's a punch line in a popular TV comedy on BBC they go into 'Unsquare Dance.' That's their bridge to the next joke."

Time Further Out also included "Charles Matthew: Hallelujah." Dave, who tends to sing themes in rhythm during an interview, remembered it this way in a conversation in his Wilton, Connecticut, home in 1992.

"It was the day our youngest son, Charles Matthew, was born. I was singing in the car all the way, from right here to the session in New York, 'Charles Matthew has been born today, Hallelujah!' [rising scale, march tempo, pounded on the table]. I got to the studio and told the guys, 'This is the theme I want to do, and we'll keep modulating because this theme doesn't seem to come back to the key I start in.' Those guys just played on that tune. There was nothing written down."

"In Your Own Sweet Way," like "Unsquare Dance," "The Duke," "Blue Rondo a la Turk," and "Take Five," has become a much-played standard—much played, not just by various Brubeck combinations, but by many other artists as well. It first appeared on *Brubeck Plays Brubeck*, recorded on April 1956. It was also played by the group at the 1956 Newport Jazz Festival and was in the *Dave Brubeck and Jay and Kai at Newport* album. In his liner note quotes for the 1993 Columbia retrospective *Time Signatures*, Dave says, "For the first few years, the Quartet played almost all standards, until one day Paul Desmond said to me, 'We've got to hire somebody to write material for us.' I said, 'Paul, are you kidding? I'll write two tunes in a half hour.' I wrote 'In Your Own Sweet Way' and 'The Waltz' that night. 'In Your Own Sweet Way' became a standard, recorded by Miles Davis, Marian McPartland, Stan Getz, Joe Pass, Bill Evans, Benny Golson, and many, many more."

During the marathon of all tours, the 1958 one that involved eighty concerts in thirteen different countries, Dave was inspired to write pieces based on phrases for "thank you" in different languages. It was *choc teshejjur ederim* in Turkish. Spoken rapidly, it became the rhythmic pattern for "The Golden Horn" (named for the narrow inlet of the Bosporus that divides Istanbul). *Dziekuje* is Polish for "thank you." And the familiar German *danke schoen* became the Bach-like "Brandenburg Gate." All these pieces were included in *Jazz Impressions of Eurasia*.

Dave has told this story about "Brandenburg Gate," composed at a time when the United States government didn't recognize East Germany, so an American entered at his own risk. To get to Poland (next destination for the Quartet), it was necessary to cross into East Germany from the Allied section of Berlin, and this was illegal without a transit visa: "In order to obtain a transit visa, I had to enter

East Germany through the Brandenburg Gate, praying that no one would question me until I had obtained the necessary papers. It was many nervous hours later that I returned back through the Brandenburg Gate to West Berlin, this time with the proper transit visa for myself and the Quartet, and a significant new title for my piece."

Dave Digs Disney (1958) and *Countdown: Time in Outer Space* (1962) provide two different versions of "Someday My Prince Will Come." In both recordings, Morello plays 4/4, Wright provides a steady 3/4, and Dave and Paul play in either 4 or 3 to take a completely different time feel. This was a total departure in jazz, and the startling fact was that it pleased the ear and teased the intellect. The public dug it almost as much as the musicians, even though it was far, far out of the mainstream.

When Brubeck began to review old sessions as Columbia Legacy and Russell Gloyd, Dave's producer, worked on the four-CD tribute, he began to notice a pattern—there would be several tracks in a row where Paul didn't play. "That was because he didn't dig the tunes," says Dave, "so I had to come up with things he'd like to make a session. Sometimes he'd like something enough to play one chorus or maybe three, but if he *really* liked it he might take ten or twelve choruses, one great idea after another. He'd just stretch out. If he didn't like it, he'd just hang his head a little, and I'd be stuck with it."

A tune Desmond dearly loved was the old Johnny Mercer-Victor Schertzinger chestnut, "Tangerine," from the 1942 film *The Fleet's In.* In the March 5, 1958, performance in Copenhagen, released originally in the album *The Dave Brubeck Quartet in Europe,* Paul opens immediately to state the melody and plays ten inspired, floating, effervescent choruses, backed by Dave's light vamping, Gene's impeccable bass, and, most of all, Joe's unadorned but totally perfect time keeping using mostly brushes. Then come five choruses from Dave, starting with one-finger, widely-spaced notes in and out of tempo. His left hand joins in for some discordant block chords, and then there's some very economic Basie-like playing to bring back Desmond. Paul gets five more choruses, interpolating bits of "White Christmas" and "La Cumparsita." Most of the way he's trading fours with Morello's brushes. A quick finale ends with a change of key.

The whole thing is a perfect example of what was best about the Classic Quartet. It was ebullient, vivacious, fired from within, and totally cohesive. You can "feel" the audience, almost holding its breath so as not to miss a thing, with applause only after solos and a stampede of an ovation at the end.

Although the Classic Quartet disbanded at the end of 1967 and only regrouped once, for a twenty-fifth-anniversary tour in 1976, its legacy remains in the Columbia recordings, many of which, as of this writing, have *never* been released and remain stashed away for the future in Columbia's famed "Iron Mountain" vaults. Those few tracks, included and released for the first time in the 1993 *Time Signatures* collection, give promise of treats to come.

But, for Paul Desmond, Eugene Wright, Joe Morello, and for Dave Brubeck new adventures in composing, playing, recording, and traveling lay just ahead.

chapter seven

Time for the Rest of the World

The luggage labels on the Brubeck Quartet's bags must have been an inch thick, plastered one over the other. They played everywhere they could, in everything from college gymnasiums to ballrooms, auditoriums to casinos. They appeared in jazz palaces like New York City's Birdland and on national television, the *Ed Sullivan Show* and Steve Allen's *Tonight,* and at a fairgrounds in Allentown, Pennsylvania, the Apollo Theatre in Harlem, and the Palladium in Hollywood.

They crisscrossed America and then went overseas. In one version or another, Dave's combos have played on every continent in the world except Antarctica.

For many years, touring was Dave's way of life. In many instances, that meant doing two programs a day, getting to the next stop, setting up and playing that night, then packing it up and going on to another city for the same routine. Dave hated it. It meant being away from Iola, a growing family, and the home he loved. To Dave, that was the heaviest price to pay for the career that was ascending steadily toward its zenith.

The tours started early in his career. They were a way to get the Brubeck sound heard, to get those odd time charts listened to, and to promote the few recordings he had made. With a devoted but small following in and around San Francisco, Brubeck needed wider exposure.

When the tours began, there was no financial backing, no management staff; making the dates, handling the transportation, doing the promotional interviews, modifying the schedule when bad weather forced layovers, handling the money, meeting the payroll—all of it was handled by Dave on the road and Iola at home. This in a time when air travel was done in planes with propellers, when trains had long since been dedicated to carrying freight instead of people, when highway rest areas had not yet been built along the road, when chains of motels had not yet been created.

But the largest problem the group faced was not getting bookings, or even getting from one place to the other. It was the racial segregation that existed as a matter of custom in much of the territory Brubeck wanted to explore as musical venues. In 1951, in the South, White and Black students did not attend the same schools, much less share classes. Blacks were assigned to the back of the bus, drank from water fountains labeled "colored," were restricted to movie theater balconies, were not allowed to eat in most restaurants, and did not share motels with Whites. In the South, Black musicians played in Black clubs, White musicians in White clubs. Audiences were similarly set apart, Whites listening to music played by Whites, Blacks to Blacks.

A Black musician in a White band was unheard of in much of the South.

On several occasions, Dave was told that, in order to get on the stage, he should get rid of Eugene Wright. He always refused, and sometimes the Quartet did not play. At one college, he was told that the Quartet could play—with Wright onstage—but the audience would have to be segregated. Again Dave refused, and the concert did not go on.

"On one tour in the South, we canceled twenty-three out of twenty-five engagements," he remembers. "That was the equivalent of half a year's work. In later years, we played most of those same Southern colleges."

In Enid, Oklahoma, the Quartet was booked for a concert, but the town's best hotel refused to give them lodging. Enid oilman Dick Knox, who liked Dave's music, heard about the problem and came up with a novel solution: "I'll just foreclose on that little ol' hotel," he said. The Quartet got the rooms.

Restaurants sometimes refused to serve them food unless Wright ate in the kitchen. Dave says "Eugene never complained. The kitchen help were almost always all Black. He ate better than we did, or any Whites did, for that matter." But the problem was not about food. It was about justice.

Much of it ended—at least on the surface—with the 1954 United States Supreme Court decision banning segregation in public schools. Succeeding decisions made racial discrimination in housing, public facilities, and transportation illegal. Dave's decency and stubbornness were vindicated.

Dave never swerved in his refusal to accept segregation. Twenty years after the battles against racism in the United States, the new Brubeck Quartet, with three Brubeck sons, faced apartheid in a 1976–77 South African tour. Dave had it stipulated in his contract that a Black, African musician would play with the Quartet in every appearance. This musician was bassist Victor N'Toni, who, in 1993, was still working with Darius Brubeck. Victor and Dave would usually play as a duo while Darius, Chris, and Danny sat out. Dave canceled two segregated concerts in Durban, but played to mixed Black and White audiences in Johannesburg and Capetown.

The years between those events were a tourist's dream—or nightmare—depending on the individual. Dave played across the world, an unofficial United States ambassador of jazz.

Sometimes it took more than diplomacy. There are mixed memories of the famous 1958 tour that the State Department sponsored, taking the Quartet to Europe, the Middle East, and the Indian sub-continent.

Turkey, he recalls, was so cold that there was ice on the inside of the airplane. Sharing the cabin with animals was a common event in some parts of that world. So were unexpected changes in the weather. "We were dressed for freezing weather when we left Turkey. When we landed in Karachi in West Pakistan, I think it was close to 120 degrees, and there we were in long underwear." The State

Department, which had organized the tour as part of the then-popular cultural exchanges, provided no escort. "There was always somebody who met you there, but they didn't care how long you had been on an airplane. They had their own agenda, and they put you right to work."

Food and other essentials posed real difficulties. "The food was OK if you're Indian, but very dangerous for an American to eat." A simple matter of getting a drink of water—"water that you could trust"—became a major problem. Dave contracted amoebic dysentery on the tour and returned home with a high fever and suffering from malnutrition.

India brought lizards, insects as big as mice or so it seemed, and more heat and humidity than the players had ever experienced. There were health problems that were helped, more or less, by vaccinations—cholera, typhoid, para-typhoid, plague. Two weeks before the tour began, their arms were jabbed repeatedly with needles, with resultant discomfort. The booster injections on the tour itself were equal impediments to flexibility.

Many in the audiences were not familiar with jazz. On that tour in 1958, the Quartet made probably the first known recording of Indian and jazz musicians improvising together. There were other occasions in Afghanistan, Turkey, and India, where Dave immersed himself in the music of the East that later influenced much of his composing. One hurdle the Quartet faced on the 1958 tour was the ban on Jewish travelers in Moslem countries. Desmond, for vague and undeclared reasons, assumed at that time he was Jewish. He went to India, but not to Iran or Iraq.

England was a joy to tour: the Quartet had never played in the huge halls of European cities. They performed in the Odeon and the Victoria theaters, which seated about three thousand people—two shows a day with sold-out crowds, concert after concert. Dave had not known that his music was that popular in England: his records filled six out of ten top jazz slots in a British popular music list. After England came the Scandinavian countries.

Five tours to Japan, nine to Australia, continuing tours to England and the Continent: the tours illustrated the curious fact that American jazz is more popular with a wider audience overseas than it is in the United States. Why is that? Ask Dave Brubeck.

CHAPTER SEVEN

"In the twenties, the Black American [musician] was much more welcome in Paris and Stockholm; they felt more free and more accepted. The radio stations in Europe play much more jazz than American stations play. The young people there have fads, but they don't throw everything else out.

"We shouldn't have our kids listening to just what they think is good. I know when I was growing up, my mother wasn't crazy about jazz. But still, she could be convinced because I could say, 'Listen to Art Tatum play 'Humoresque.' Then I could connect with her.

"There's nothing to connect a lot of what's going on today with . . . of our past culture. We need to save the good from the past. Kids will tell me they don't know what jazz is; what's scary about that is, they're hearing it all day long on TV, and they don't know that what they're hearing is jazz—so many commercials, so many background scores from movies written by people like Pete Rugolo or Quincy Jones. The kids are exposed, but they know so little it's like they're getting an automobile and it's the first one they've ever seen. They don't know about the wheel or the buggy or anything getting them up to the present time.

"In Europe, they have a sense of history. The people who come to jazz concerts know what it is. I think we're starting to catch up with that."

The message that he was carrying through the United States and Europe was not just jazz, but new ways to think about and to play music. The way to spread the word was in person—playing a schedule of almost-daily engagements (on many days multiple concerts) in schools, concert halls, fairgrounds, colleges, night clubs, and dance halls. It was a schedule that was almost impossible then, and is almost impossible now, but the group did it.

One particular year stands out. The Dave Brubeck Quartet's Great World Tour, some might call it, started in the Blackhawk in San Francisco on January 2, 1958, and ended on December 31 at the Palladium in Hollywood. There were 125 different engagements in thirty-seven different cities in fourteen countries from England to Iraq.

There were many hairy, scary times during that marathon tour, but the visit to Poland—the first of many—was like something out of Eric Ambler or John LeCarre. Eugene Wright gives a detailed recollection of what happened: "We went through East Germany with no visas, no State Department escort, no nothin'. We were on purely the blessings of those people. To get to Poland, we started in West Berlin where they loaded us into these army trucks. I'm in one truck by myself with my bass. We get to the checkpoint to go through East Germany, and this Russian guard has a machine gun, and he has it pointed right at me. Me being Black confused him a little, but he finally let us through the Brandenburg Gate. We got to the train station in East Berlin. None of the people there—nice people—had ever seen anything like me and my bass fiddle. We got aboard OK. But we stopped every hour, give or take, at a checkpoint. They'd go through the train with machine guns at each end of the car, and they would say to each person, 'namanee.' I thought they were talking about money. I had no money, just travelers' checks. They asked me over and over, 'namanee, namanee, namanee,' and got all excited. Finally, one of them said 'passport,' and I showed them mine, and we went on.

"At last we got to Poland, and we got off. It was like one of those spy movies with the single light hanging down on a cord from above in a shanty that had dirt floors, where we had to wait for the bus. This was wintertime, and it was *cold*. Finally, the bus got there. Some bus! It was a 1923 model with wooden floors, lots of holes where the wood had broken through. We had to drive all night to Stettin, where we were scheduled to play. There was no heater. It was the longest, coldest night I've ever known.

"We got there in the morning and thawed out and checked in at the hotel. They wouldn't pick up our bags, and I said, 'I'll tip 'em.' and the manager said, 'Don't do that. If you tip, and they don't report it, they'll be shot.' The hotel, like everything around it, was still full of holes and being rebuilt after the wartime bombing, but we could get some sleep and play the concert.

"Next stop was Warsaw to play with the symphony orchestra, and the lady who met us was sort of in charge. She took us to her house where she had this big concert grand. Not much heat, not much food, but a beautiful concert grand. And she played and she played. Dave and I looked at each other. It was so beautiful it really got to you. She wanted Dave to play, but he just wanted to listen to her.

"The concert, of course, was sold out. It was a big, old auditorium that missed being bombed, and they loved us. I met a lot of the orchestra members, especially the bass players, and we just talked music. The people, all the people, were very nice, but, boy, were they poor. At that time they just didn't have anything. Hearing us—American jazz, all the way from America—was like a feast for them. They couldn't believe it.

"The next day I went to a church in Warsaw, built in the fifteenth century. I wanted to go to mass. Inside the church there were figurines all over the place. When the organ started playing, those figurines started *moving!* When we went in, the church was just as cold inside as it was outside, but when the Mass started, it was no longer cold. I don't know why; I still can't explain it. They told me it was bombed all around there, but somehow this church was missed."

The Polish tour took the Quartet on to Danzig, Lodz, Kraków, and Poznan. The group found beauty amidst destruction everywhere, and everywhere rebuilding was under way. So well were they received and so many friends were made that Dave brought the group back three times in later years.

At the time of the first Poland concert tour, they were unable to go into the Soviet Union, but that permission materialized years later. How it happened is a mixture of music and diplomacy, according to Brubeck's manager, Russell Gloyd, who gives the following detailed account.

"In 1983, harpsichordist Igor Kipnis, a neighbor of the Brubecks in Wilton, was in Moscow playing a concert as part of a series of American artists performing in Spasso House, the American embassy. At that time, three years after President Carter had boycotted United States participation in the 1980 Moscow Olympic Games because of the Soviet army's invasion of Afghanistan, there were no official cultural exchanges between the United States and U.S.S.R. The U.S. ambassador, talking to Kipnis, mentioned how good it would be to have Dave Brubeck there. Kipnis, who was Dave's neighbor, promised to talk to Dave about it.

"A series of conversations brought us to a point where we would play at the embassy in Moscow in 1984. We had our visas, everything was set up, and then it was canceled because of the Korean airliner attack. So we scheduled it again, this time for a concert at Spasso House in Moscow and a second concert in Leningrad. We had a call from the ambassador, who said he had just learned that the KGB

[Soviet secret police] was going to put a ring around the embassy and that everyone coming to the performance would be subject to arrest or to losing their privileges. He recommended that the trip be canceled.

"This was the first time we had any indication of how popular Dave Brubeck was in the Soviet Union—that people would risk their future just to be able to hear him in person.

"In 1985, President Reagan met with Premier Gorbachev in Geneva—the first post-Khrushchev summit. The president flew back to the United States, and that night he announced to Congress that the first thing agreed upon was establishing a new cultural exchange treaty. The next day, I fired off a letter to our ambassador. Now the State Department and USIA get into it—the typical government thing, where they talk a lot and not much happens. The scene now shifts to September 1986; I am in Paris, and I get a call at the hotel from the Soviets: 'Please come to our embassy, we have some very important messages for you.' It informed me that the head of GosConcert, the official concert agency of the Soviet Union, wanted me to come from Paris to Moscow for meetings regarding a Dave Brubeck tour.

"This was Wednesday; on Friday I go to the Soviet embassy in Paris. Normally, it takes three weeks to get a visa; I had mine in an hour. Tuesday I flew to Moscow. All I knew was I had a visa valid for two cities for five days. I was taken to our embassy the next morning, and talked with GosConcert the next day. They started off wanting ten concerts in Moscow in a seventeen-thousand-seat arena. I said we wanted to come to Moscow, but that we were coming as strangers, and we wanted to leave as friends. I said you cannot do that in a seventeen-thousand-seat arena; you must do that in a concert hall. They said, 'Well, you know Mr. Brubeck already has his friends here.' I said that was good and that we would like to keep them as friends.

"The upshot was that we agreed to have five concerts in Moscow, five in Leningrad, and three in Tallinn, all in concert halls seating three or four thousand. My translator, it turned out, was a theater person; she really wasn't aware of Dave. She saw me later on that day and said, 'What you have arranged is terrible. No one will be able to get tickets. I have checked on your Mr. Brubeck, and he is so well known that no one will be able to get tickets except the bureaucracy. That is as far as the tickets would go.'"

But as things turned out, the translator underestimated the determination of Brubeck fans. Gloyd remembers the tour, with Dave, son Chris, Bill Smith, and Randy Jones, as incredible. The reception was overwhelming. When Dave went to the Composers Club next to Tchaikovsky Hall, ostensibly to meet with Moscow composers and musicians, the police had to block off the street because hundreds of people had gathered just to see Dave, people who would have no chance of getting inside. It was a mob scene like at a rock concert. There were three hundred to four hundred people at the theater every night just hoping to get tickets that might have been turned back.

"And this was in what was supposedly cold and impersonal Moscow. Everyone was saying, 'Just forget about Moscow, it's going to be five concerts of bureaucratic people in the audience, with no response. It will only be when you leave Moscow that you'll get the real people.' This we found to be absolutely untrue. The final Moscow concert we videotaped on A&E—you hear an audience that was just beside itself."

By the time the tour reached Leningrad, ticket demand was so great that the performance had to be switched to a sports stadium. The final concert was, Gloyd says, "one of the most exciting nights of our lives."

That was in 1985, but Dave's constant caravaning from city to city and state to state had begun more than twenty years before. Despite the exhilaration and audience response the tours brought, Dave had always found them exhausting.

As early as 1959, he had been ready to end the big-name music career and settle down in San Francisco to play local gigs. One thing kept him traveling: he was broke. The concerts had produced a lot of revenue, but it all went in expenses. After his attorney told him he actually owed ten thousand dollars in federal taxes, Dave knew the price of fame. A solution was found: one final move, taking his family along, from California to Connecticut, closer to the places that were opening to promote the sound of "West Coast jazz" that Brubeck had carried across the country—indeed, across the world. In Wilton, Connecticut, Dave Brubeck would finally find home.

From there, the tours continued, but at nowhere near the frenetic pace of 1958.

And now it's 1995. Would he tour again? In a minute, but he would limit the number of concerts and space them to accommodate his health and energy limitations. He first mentions Russia, "if it settled down politically," and next, Poland, "I've been to Poland four times, I'd like to go back again." The list grows: "There's a great bass player in Czechoslovakia, Pegi, a gypsy—he's like a Charlie Mingus. I love to play in Germany, and Austria is probably the most musical audience there is; they are so ready for the music, and they seem to know what's good. One time we got six encores, and the promoter said, 'You have to get off the stage or it's going to cost me another $3,500.' So we got off, took off our tuxes, put on our street clothes, and he came into the dressing room and said, 'They won't leave. If you don't go out there, I might have more than $3,500 to pay because they're getting pretty raucous.' So we went out and played again in our street clothes."

In Berlin, at the Berlin Philharmonic, the Quartet (with Gerry Mulligan) had to go back on in street clothes, too. It happened often. An audience that kept applauding for a half-hour after the concert was officially over, encores and all, could not be denied.

European audiences telegraph their message of appreciation to the performers more than Americans do. The performers feed on the energy.

"When you hit the stage, *Pow!*" says Dave. "You *know.*"

Most of the touring concerts were done without a program. Sometimes the Quartet didn't know where the music would lead or who would be doing what riffs on what tunes. They would wait to see where the music would take them. The performances were like living history to serious music students because they recreated the spontaneity of baroque compositions which were often improvised by the composer who wrote the music down after it had been played before an audience.

The Dave Brubeck Quartet spent most of the next ten years on the road, in intensive concertizing separated by periods of rest. The playing was always professional, but at times, weariness would take its toll. A late arriving plane would put the Quartet onstage without dinner or time to shave, just time enough to change into tuxedos and go out before four thousand cheering fans who probably didn't notice the five o'clock shadow because of their enthusiasm for the music.

The membership changed during that time, with drummer Joe Morello coming aboard in 1956 and shifting the musical emphasis. As a Brubeck Quartet member, Joe Morello won *Down Beat* polls and *Playboy* polls and international popularity awards in what became annual routines—the only non-leader drummer who could claim that distinction.

Touring brought the group together, overcoming even Desmond's legendary impatience with drummers. The schedules became less arduous. Now the drill was one month on the road, a series of dates in town for the next month, then a month off. The time off included occasional rehearsals. But the easier schedule still kept Dave away from his family for longer stretches of time than he cared for.

Sometimes, they would forget where they had played the night before. And the audiences wanted more and more. It was, as Morello recalls, the best small jazz ensemble playing at that time, and the playing made it all better. Joe remembers that "the colleges were the best places to play because after the sets, the kids would come up onstage and talk to us. About fifty drummers would be talking to me about technique and what kind of drums—I felt kind of sorry for Paul because no one was asking him what kind of reed to use— but I would be the last guy out of there."

When playing colleges, the Quartet was invariably invited to receptions and parties before and after the concert. The socializing was fun, but it also required energy that playing and touring had already tapped. The group would flip a coin to see who would go, who would talk it up with the crowd.

For the Quartet, the travel and the concerts are remembered with mixed feelings. As Morello put it, "Where else are you going to get paid to go around the world a few times? Where else can you get paid for doing what you would be doing anyway?" But as the touring continued, the toll it exacted inevitably became more onerous. In 1966, Dave finally told the Quartet that the following year would be its last. The Quartet recorded its farewell session on November 13, 1967, in Paris. A few gigs followed, and Dave returned home to rest, study, and seek new directions for his music.

The hiatus lasted one month. "George Wein [a longtime

promoter and producer of jazz festivals] called me and he said, 'I need you, Dave, in Mexico. They won't take the festival unless you come. You're gonna put a lot of guys out of work unless you sign on!' George had done a lot of favors for me. He really helped me get started. I thought, 'What am I gonna do for a quartet?' George said, 'I've got Gerry Mulligan already hired.' I replied, 'I've got Jack Six, who's a great bass player'—he had sight read my oratorio, *Light in the Wilderness,* and played it at its premiere.

"When it came to drummers, George said, 'There's a lot of good drummers,' and I said, 'Yeah, but are there a lot of good *guys?'* A couple of hours later, we had Alan Dawson, thanks to George's wife, Joyce. And Alan met *both* qualifications."

In May 1968, this new Quartet, with Gerry Mulligan, was playing in Mexico City. Mulligan, by the way, was an old friend from the Blackhawk days who was destined to be partnered with Dave on many occasions into the mid-nineties. The Mexican audience had worshiped the Brubeck sound in its earlier Quartet modes, primarily through the album called *Bravo Brubeck,* in which Mexican musicians played with the Quartet without rehearsal or scores, and the result had a kick like Mexican chilies. This was Dave's third musical journey to Mexico.

One album, *Compadres,* came from this Mexican trip, containing both Brubeck and Mulligan compositions written for the tour. There were two concerts in Guadalajara and then, with no further rehearsal, came the time to record the album. The four players sound as if they had been together for years, though they had never played together before being assembled by Wein.

One of the tunes, "Indian Song," carried reminders of Dave's childhood association with a Native American cowboy. The rhythms were established with Alan Dawson playing a maraca in one hand while playing the snare drum, and Mulligan and Six played strong roles as well.

So good was the result that the four stayed together, constituting a new Dave Brubeck Quartet—a more mature group than the first, one that observed the human limits of endurance with a lighter travel schedule and one that required fewer responsibilities for Brubeck himself.

Time for Compatriots: I

Although the formal continuum of the Dave Brubeck Quartet should be recorded as 1951 to the end of 1967, the golden years clearly began in 1958, when Eugene Wright joined Joe Morello, Paul Desmond, and Dave, forming a group that began nearly ten years of unparalleled creative activity. Its greatest expression came in the international tours, concerts at prestigious venues and, most fully, on recordings. The DBQ won the *Down Beat* readers' poll in '59, '62, '63, '64, and '65. It topped *Billboard*'s disc jockey poll in '62 and the reader's poll in '65 and '66. It was crowned winner of the *Playboy* readers' poll for twelve consecutive years, '57 through '68.

Quite simply, the Dave Brubeck Quartet was the most successful of all organized, touring, recording jazz groups in the 1960s. Of any jazz group, the Quartet reached the widest popular audience in terms of age, education, and musical interests. What is a little difficult to establish is why.

Part of the answer lies in what the Quartet was *not*. It was not bop-derivative, paying little homage to Charlie Parker's figures or Dizzy Gillespie's excursions. Remember that this was a time when about 90 percent of all White groups (and many Black as well) were as, Brubeck says, "chasing each other's tails." It was not West Coast cool, even though the earlier and experimental Octet recordings Dave made were tightly arranged and classical-modern in concept. The Quartet was not built solely on original compositions. Although its biggest success, *Time Out,* was an album of originals, the group's main fare consisted of standards. It was able to, and often did, swing hard. The music was even danceable.

With Dave Brubeck and Paul Desmond creating the voices, listeners were immediately and viscerally connected to familiar songs touched with harmonic and rhythmic textures that, luckily, they found intriguing. After the voices of Eugene Wright and Joe Morello were added as a fixed half of the group, they became far more than the rhythm section, solid and sure as they were in the necessary underpinnings.

All this was presented with the utmost enthusiasm of a still-shy young Brubeck, even before he was able to bring himself to talk directly to his audiences. In action, uninhibited when in working tandem with his piano, his eyes widened and flashed with the intensity of the moment, especially during some particularly inspired innovation of a particular solo. He would sneak glances at the audience as they too became caught up in the heat of the performance, and their obvious pleasure would fuel his creative fires. The leader's joy was the spark that turned a small club or a vast auditorium into a combustion chamber. Not surprisingly, some of the Quartet's best recordings were those done at concerts.

Trying to explain the international success of the Quartet, Brubeck says simply, "It's hard to pin down. I guess we were just able to *communicate.*" The underlying reasons also probably rest with the individual personalities and their compatibilities, despite vast differences in background, experience, and training.

Bassist Eugene Wright puts it this way: "It was a beautiful marriage, because each person had his part to do and did it in harmony. Joe Morello and I were 'The Section,' and when we hit the stand we meant business. It was nice because bass and drums should always be together. That left Dave the freedom to do what he wanted and Paul the freedom to do what *he* wanted. Once in a lifetime do you work with somebody ten or fifteen years and never have an argument, never have a fuss. Dave and I never had a run-in or an argument, never had a misunderstanding. It was friendship plus playing, and it was the same way with Joe Morello.

"Joe was one of my closest friends. And Paul Desmond was a beautiful man. I've seen him do things on the outside you wouldn't believe, like paying the hospital bills and helping out all kinds of people he hardly knew. He was a giant. They were *all* giants! So many people, for instance, don't know Dave's full potential. That man knows the Tatum school and all the schools of piano. He can play them all."

Wright also says that he has no regrets about it having ended. "It was a great ten years. I had a ball, mainly because of Dave and Iola and Joe and Paul. That was the era of my life I was blessed to have. If you listen to the music of today, it's traveled in a whole different direction. If somebody calls me to do something I don't like to do, I say no. Jack Six [who often worked with Brubeck in the eighties and nineties] is the right player for now. Dave is moving forward all the time. He ain't playing what were playing back then! But when he calls me to play, it's because he wants to play the kind of things we used to play for a particular situation. And then it's a ball all over again!"

Eugene Joseph Wright, better known among fans and fellow musicians as "Senator," was born in Chicago, May 29, 1923. He studied cornet in school and taught himself string bass. By 1943 he had his own group, the Dukes of Swing, jobbing about his home-town. He jammed with the likes of Charlie Parker, Sonny Stitt, and Gene Ammons and in 1949 and 1950 was with the Count Basie Band. Then came a tour with Arnett Cobb and a long one (1952–1955) with Buddy DeFranco which brought Gene to California, followed by stints with Red Norvo and Cal Tjader.

Gene is a big, gentle, patient, intelligent, and articulate man who can play (and *does* play) everything from Dixieland to straight-ahead Swing to the sophisticated counter-rhythms that the Brubeck Quartet came to represent. He considers his role as that of the solid underpinning—steady and swinging. With the Quartet, he often doubled as a road manager, responsible for getting men and instruments intact to the right place at the right time. Along the way, Senator Wright collected friends in every corner of the world, with whom he continued to correspond through the years. Families from Germany to Australia with whom Gene became close during tours have made him a godfather many times over.

It's no wonder that Wright became and continues to be a teacher, both privately and at schools. He was chairman of the jazz department at the University of Cincinnati and head of the advisory board in the jazz division of the International Society of Bassists.

Considering his success in making friends overseas, you'd expect a nickname like "Ambassador" rather than "Senator" for Eugene Wright. The appellation has nothing to do with public office, which Wright never sought. According to Joe Morello, they were on a plane somewhere in Europe. "We were making up phony languages, just to pass the time, and when the stewardess came by and heard this strange, crazy talk, I translated for her. 'The senator from Bulgaria would like a cup of coffee.' Somehow this became a standing gag, but Gene first became aware that the name had been codified like the "Duke" in Ellington or the "Count" in Basie when the group arrived in Ceylon. Gene, as usual, was the first Quartet member to check in, responsible as he was for all the instruments and transportation. He remembers, "I'm coming in the door and the manager says to me, 'Good evening, Senator, welcome to Ceylon.'" Next thing he knew, Iola sent him an airline ticket for "Senator Eugene Wright and his instrument," and the airline staff treated him like royalty, rushing him and his bass (he always had to book two seats) into first class. So as a result of the gag, Wright became known by his assumed title from the State Department tour of 1958 onward.

Senator Wright lives in North Hollywood, California. His wife, Phyllis, is an actress and a director, and Gene himself has appeared in numerous television shows. He has a number of students and, when the gig is pleasurable, he plays clubs and concerts. Many of his compositions are in his book, *Modern Music for Bass*, which was brought out by Charles Hansen Publications.

It was drummer Joe Morello who first suggested Wright to Brubeck as the 1958 world tour approached and the bassist, Norman Bates, didn't want to leave his home for the extended period. Gene was a little reluctant. His professional beginnings date back to the old Basie band in '49. "I told Dave I didn't know what he was playing or if I could play what Dave was playing." But when the two got together and began playing "Brother, Can You Spare a Dime?" and a few other old goodies he liked to play, Gene realized that they both loved to swing. He said, "Well, if you're happy, Dave, I'm happy. OK, I'll do it." Thus a Black bass player out of Chicago joined an Indian-Caucasian pianist out of Concord. It was, as Gene says, "A happy marriage from the word 'go.'"

The first continental United States date for the Quartet, following the hiring of Wright, was at a White college in Georgia.

Wright now states, "I won't say the name—that way nobody'll get hurt. Let's just say we got to the college. And the dean said to Dave, 'You can play. But Mr. Wright can't go on.'"

Dave said, "What do you mean he can't go on?"

"Well, you know that's forbidden."

"Wait a minute. I'm not going to play this town if I can't use my group. Gene Wright's with my group. Now if you don't want my bass player to play with my group, then we won't play at all."

It went from dean to mayor to governor; this had never happened before. And meantime, students packing the auditorium had found out what was happening. They began stamping their feet in support of Wright playing. The concert had been delayed an hour and a half before the final decision was made.

"Then," Wright explains, "we hit that stand and started playing! And, boy, that place—well, it was one of the best of concerts. We just had a ball!"

Dave's response to that situation had hardly been planned. By nature and by example, he is a hater of bigotry. But he did prove by his actions that evening that when he took on a musician he also took on the *man* who was that musician. Loyalty can be rewarded by loyalty. Which is what Wright bestowed upon the man who hadn't let him down that night in the South. There's little doubt that such loyalties can be reflected in the music played by the Quartet. Says Gene Wright today: "After about three more years, Dave realized he had a rhythm section that allowed him the freedom to play those time things he loved. That's why everything we did came off beautifully. That Quartet was so tight because Joe and I could start cooking and, man, if Dave decided to let us stroll, Paul Desmond could set up ninety thousand choruses. It was, yeah, what we called a beautiful marriage."

Two years earlier, in 1956, Dave Brubeck had hired Joe Morello, of Springfield, Massachusetts, to be his drummer. Says Dave, "The character of the group changed when Joe Morello joined us. He's the best in the world for complex rhythms."

Nearly blind from birth, Morello revealed his capabilities as a musician as a child, playing both piano and violin. He compensated for his limited vision by memorizing the music. But his greatest love was percussion. It wasn't until Morello was interviewed on National Public Radio in late 1993 to plug a new album of his that the public learned just how proficient he had been as a violinist. At about age nine, he played the full Mendelssohn Violin Concerto in Boston's Symphony Hall with members of the Boston Pops. Joe was reticent about talking about this period, saying, "Not long after, through a friend, I met Jascha Heifetz. After meeting and talking with him and listening to him play, I pretty much put the violin away forever." Dave Brubeck, hearing about the NPR interview during the research for this book, commented, "I worked with him night and day, all over the world, for all those years, and he never told me that story!"

Morello's mother took him to a drum instructor when he was fourteen. In addition to the formal instruction, he sharpened his skills by going to the Court Square Theater, a vaudeville house in his home town. He would sit in the front row and watch the drummer play in the pit. More than once, a performer in one of the acts would look down at him and say, "Hey, the show's up here, buddy!" Listening to radio remotes of the time is what honed his interest in playing jazz. He found inspiration from a wide range of drummers that included Sidney Catlett, Jo Jones, Chick Webb, and Buddy Rich. In time, he began playing professionally by gigging around with local hotel bands on weekends. He worked his way to New York as part of a corny commercial trio. It was there that Marian McPartland, playing at the Hickory House, invited him to sit in. Says McPartland, "He looked less like a drummer than a student of nuclear physics—the guy with the diffident air. He was gentle and quiet, then extrovertish, then moody. He had a precise blending of touch, taste, and an almost unbelievable technique."

Morello became a member of McPartland's group. Dave, who once told Marian that she was one of his three favorite pianists (the others were Teddy Wilson and Art Tatum) used to hang out at the

CHAPTER EIGHT

Hickory House when he was in town and had time. There he heard Morello. Marian says, with a laugh, "He stole him away."

"Dave and I were talking at the Park Sheraton," Morello would remember. "I told Dave, 'You don't feature the drums at all. And I like to play a little bit. Let's try it for a month.'"

Once in Brubeck's Quartet, Morello demonstrated not only polished virtuosity and marked creativity, but also flourished in the band's studied sense of time. In fact, Morello proved himself to be not only a master of the art of time-playing, but also to be a flashy, crowd-pleasing drummer, a situation not unnoticed by saxophonist Paul Desmond, who'd been with Brubeck since the forties. Desmond, in his own estimation, was the star sideman, a reasonable judgment based upon the man's demonstrated genius.

Crowds cheered Brubeck's rhythmic key-pounding as they did Morello's stickwork. On the other hand, some of Desmond's most intricate lines got only subdued appreciation.

At the Blue Note in Chicago, the situation blew up. The crowds were good. On the first night Brubeck featured Morello with a drum solo. The performance got a standing ovation. Desmond walked offstage to his dressing room. When Brubeck joined him there, Desmond said, "Either Morello leaves or I do." Brubeck, always certain in his role as a leader, replied, "Morello stays."

Desmond did not leave. But the relationship between him and Morello was strained for some time. During the college tours, Morello got to be quite celebrated. Perhaps fifteen young drummers would be asking Morello to show them this or show them that. Few would ask Paul Desmond for advice. Paul and Morello hardly talked to one another.

But Morello, who won the *Down Beat* poll five years in a row and the *Playboy* poll for seven years, tried hard to play and get along as best he could. He sensed that Desmond was gradually giving in to the situation during an evening concert at the Summer Theater in New Jersey. Morello was featured alone onstage with a ten-minute drum solo during "Take Five." Desmond had gone backstage where he'd seated himself with, characteristically, a paperback collection of Dostoevski short stories. There he remarked, wearily, about the number, "It was supposed to be a drum solo, but it wasn't supposed to be a hit record." It's not certain if fires were rekindled when

Brubeck also credited Morello with having been largely responsible for creating the 5/4 rhythm of "Take Five." What is certain is that after Gene Wright joined the band, his presence made all the difference in relationships as well as in performance.

Says Joe Morello today, "As time went on, Paul and I got to be very, very close friends. We hung out together the last four or five years of the group."

The symbiosis between personal relationships and musical relationships developed to the point of artistic intuitiveness. Brubeck called the shots and calibrated the limits. Desmond fueled the fires of innovation. Wright and Morello were what they always called themselves, "The Section"—the never-failing rhythmic underpinning. And Joe Morello was clearly a Rock of Gibraltar—two hands, two feet, capable Wright remembers of playing four different rhythms at the same time. Wright, who says he learned a lot from guitarist Freddie Green and drummer Jo Jones while with Basie, points out, "First thing is you listen to your partner. Listen to his bass drum, no matter what else he may be doing, and play with that. Boy, did I learn from Joe Morello!"

To his fellow Quartet members and to his friends, Paul Desmond was an enigma. His soaring talent aside, he was a man on whom it was not easy to pin labels. When talking to some of those who knew him best, certain perceived characteristics recur. He was a sardonic loner, a womanizer, and collector of pornography who had, at the same time, a very puritanical streak. He was, they say, terribly proper but also sensual. As writer Gene Lees says, "He hated daylight. He was a creature of the nighttime. He was the loneliest man I ever knew."

Born November 25, 1924, in San Francisco, his name was Paul Emil Breitenfeld, later changed to Paul Desmond, a name chosen for its Irishness from a phone book. In fact, his mother was Irish, his father a German who worked as an organist in the San Francisco theaters. According to his friends, Paul somehow came to believe he was Jewish. It's not clear if that was the reason for his adopting "Desmond" as a career move. It did keep him from appearing with the Quartet in such countries as Iran and Iraq. Toward the end of his life, however, Paul decided he was *not* of Jewish descent on his father's side—another twist in a complicated personality.

Among the Quartet members, Paul was the only very heavy

CHAPTER EIGHT

drinker. He was an extremely heavy smoker as well, an addiction that eventually cost him his life. The drinking never interfered with his professional life when he was committed to a gig, a tour, or a record date. The smoking, on the other hand, was sometimes a problem for Dave and Gene Wright, who usually managed to travel together while Paul and Joe Morello took a separate car when they were on the road.

Although Desmond achieved enormous popularity, Gene Lees explains, "He was very underrated by the critical establishment because he was Californian, he was White, and because he came from the comfortable middle class." But Brubeck knew what a star he had in Desmond and gave him 15 percent of the royalties on all Brubeck recordings that included Paul. Those royalties continued to be paid to his estate after his death. If he were alive today, he'd be quite a rich man. His estate, by the way, went to the Red Cross, a bequest that greatly puzzled those close to him since he had never shown any particular interest in that organization.

Desmond's style and tone were unmistakably his. He was trained as a pianist, then studied clarinet, tenor sax, and alto sax. Gene Lees believes Paul's truly exquisite tone on the alto came out of listening to Lester Young's clarinet playing. There was a delicate, caressing quality, and Brubeck cultivated that and also exploited the knowledge that Paul played best when he was angry. Knowing that Desmond hated up-tempo things, Dave would often open a set with a barnburner, such as "Let's Get Away from It All," to which Paul responded with a force that matched his lyricism. Lees says it was a "pas de deux. Dave knew what to feed Paul and when."

Dave tried to get Paul to compose more often, but it was very difficult. He was perhaps too critical of everything, including his own work. He told Gene Lees, "I'd find myself constantly taking a tinier screwdriver to every phrase, and I could never finish a single piece." That applied to his writing at the typewriter, too. Desmond would have liked to have been successful at that, more than anything. He constantly carried his typewriter with him. He started a book and had a great title: "How Many of You Are There in the Quartet." He got just one chapter done. Dave says, "He just couldn't face other people reading what he thought they'd criticize. He just couldn't get past himself."

The single completed chapter from Paul's projected book was titled "How Jazz Came to Orange County State Fair." This refers to New Jersey's Orange County, not California's. It was published in the January 10, 1973, edition of *Punch*. From all accounts, it perfectly captures that bittersweet, sardonic quality of Paul's self-effacing humor. We excerpt it here:

> DAWN. A station wagon pulls up to the office of an obscure motel in New York. Three men enter: pasty-faced, grim-eyed, silent (for those are their names). Perfect opening shot, before credits, for a really lousy bank-robbery movie? Wrong. The Dave Brubeck Quartet, some years ago, starting our day's work.
>
> Today we have a contract (an offer we should have refused) for two concerts at the Orange County State Fair in Middletown. 2 p.m. and 8 p.m. Brubeck likes to get to the job early.
>
> So we pull up behind this hay truck around noon, finally locating the guy who had signed the contract. Stout, rednecked, gruff and harried (from the old New York law firm of the same name) and clearly more comfortable judging cattle than booking jazz groups. He peers into the station wagon, which contains four musicians, bass, drums, and assorted baggage and for the first and only time in our seventeen years of wandering about the world we get this question: "Where's the piano?"
>
> So, leaving Brubeck to cope with the situation, we head into town for sandwiches and browsing. Since sandwiches take more time than browsing, I pick up a copy of the Middletown Record and things become a bit more clear. TEENAGERS' DAY AT THE ORANGE COUNTY STATE FAIR, says the headline across the two center pages. Those poor folk thought we were this red-hot teenage attraction, which Lord knows we've never been. Our basic audience begins with creaking elderly types of twenty-three and above.
>
> So, now realizing, in Brubeck's piquant ranch phrase, "which way the hole slopes," we head back to the fairgrounds where the scene is roughly as follows: there is a smallish, almost transistorized, oval race track. (I'm not exactly sure how long a furlong is, but it seems not too many of them are actually present). On the side of the oval is the grandstand, built to accommodate 2,000 or so, occupied at the moment by eight or nine elderly folk who clearly paid their money to sit in the shade and fan themselves, as opposed to any burning desire to hear the music their teenage grandchildren everywhere thrill to.
>
> Directly across the track from them is our bandstand: a wooden

platform, about ten foot high and immense. Evidently no piano has been locatable in Orange County, since the only props on the stage are a vintage electric organ and one mike. Behind us is a fair-sized tent containing about two hundred people, in which a horse show for young teenagers is currently in progress, scheduled, we soon discover, to continue throughout our concert. This is hazardous mainly because their sound system is vastly superior to ours.

So we begin our desperation opener, "St. Louis Blues." Brubeck, who never spent more than ten minutes of his life at an electric organ, much less the one he is now at, sounds like an early Atwater-Kent Synthesizer. Eugene Wright, our noble bass player and me take turns schlepping the mike back and forth between us and playing grouchy, doomed choruses, but the only sound we can hear comes from our friendly neighborhood horse show.

"LOPE" it roars, "CANTER . . . TROT . . . AND THE WINNER IN THE TWELVE-YEAR-OLD CLASS IS . . . JACQUELINE HIGGS!"

As always in difficult situations such as these, we turn to our main man, primo virtuoso of the group, the Maria Callas of the drums, Joe Morello, who has rescued us from disaster from Grand Forks to Rajkot, India.

"You got it," we said, "stretch out," which ordinarily is like issuing a travel card to a hijacker. And, to his eternal credit, Morello outdoes himself. All cymbals sizzling, all feet working (Morello has several. Not many people know this). Now he's into the triplets around the tom-toms, which have shifted foundations from the Odeon Hammersmith to Free Trade Hall and have turned Buddy Rich greener than usual with envy.

The horse show is suddenly silent. Fanning in the stands has subsided slightly.

Suddenly a figure emerges from the horse tent, hurtles to the side of the stage, and yells at Brubeck, "For Chrissakes, could you tell the drummer not to play so loud? He's terrifying the horses."

Later, four pasty-faced, grim-eyed men pile into a station wagon and drive away. It may not be bank-robbery, but it's a living.

There's more to the story as written by Paul, but Dave says he forgot one thing: "Every time Paul would hit a high note on the sax, a rooster in the poultry shed would crow."

As to the title of the projected Desmond book on the Quartet, Paul explained it this way. "At least once, and usually more often, a month, we'd get on a plane and, first would come Gene Wright with his bass. Then came Joe Morello—Dr. Cyclops, although he was always good-natured about his thick glasses. This procession would alert the flight attendants and passengers that something was happening.

"First the salesman in the second row behind Gene with the bass would say, 'Hey, are you going to tuck it under your chin and play some music for us?' That was inevitable. Then the stewardess would say, 'What band are you with?' And we'd say, 'Well, actually it's the Dave Brubeck Quartet.' In the earlier days they would then say, 'Oh?', meaning much the same thing. Then, when the flight got comfortably under way, and they had some leisure, the stewardess would come back and sit down and say, 'How many of you are there in the quartet?'" A title was born.

The breakup of the celebrated Quartet came at the end of 1967 and signaled a radical departure in the life-style of Paul Desmond. He just flat-out quit playing and led an indolent existence with lots of beautiful women (mostly models), lots of booze, and much hanging-out with writer friends at Elaine's, a bar on New York's upper East Side. A frequent companion at that time was Doug Ramsey, who did the absolutely superb liner notes for the four-CD Columbia collection, *Dave Brubeck: Time Signatures*. Doug's impression was that Desmond welcomed a long rest, that he was worn out from the incessant traveling and concertizing. He'd play his black Steinway grand in his penthouse apartment at Fifty-sixth Street and Sixth Avenue, but no jam sessions took place there. Paul listened to lots of music, but there was no participation on his part. Ramsey remembers going with him to a place called Reno Sweeny's, where Blossom Dearie and Bill Evans were appearing. "Bill and Paul and I were sitting, talking, when Bill said, 'Gee, would you please sit in?' Paul said, 'No, I don't think I'd like to do that.' I offered to go back to his apartment and get his sax for him, and Bill said, somewhat plaintively, 'Well, gee, Lee [Konitz] sat in last week.' Paul was unmoved and refused to play."

The long layoff finally ended when (through the intervention of Gene Lees) Paul Grosney offered Desmond a gig at Bourbon Street in Toronto. This would put Paul in the position of leader, a major departure. Lees suggested Don Thompson on bass, Ed Bickert on

CHAPTER EIGHT

guitar, and either Terry Clark or Jerry Fuller on drums. Desmond tried both and settled on Fuller, a somewhat less-busy player. It worked well. The gig was a triumph for the group and led to some excellent live recordings. Paul hung out with Janet and Gene Lees and came back to New York feeling triumphant about the whole thing.

There were other engagements, including one at the new Half Note (into which Paul could practically fall from his apartment), a featured spot at the 1969 New Orleans JazzFest with Gerry Mulligan, and a number of recordings for various labels.

Then, in 1976, the idea of a twenty-fifth anniversary tour came up and, to Dave Brubeck's surprise, Gene Wright, Joe Morello, *and* Paul all embraced the project. This was eight years after all had agreed it was time to get off the road.

They did fifteen cities in twenty-five days by bus. Paul even wrote some notes for the souvenir program, remembering his first meeting with Brubeck.

> It was early in 1944. I was in an Army band in San Francisco; he was on his way overseas as a rifleman. Although, as is his custom, he soon ended up with his own band, touring Germany with the Rockettes and ultimately sleeping in Hermann Goering's bed (Goering, I hasten to add, was not actually present at the time).
>
> That afternoon, though, he was straight off the ranch: hawk-faced, suspicious and quick-moving, engulfed in a fleece-lined purple jacket. We got together with a few other musicians and played for about a half an hour. "Rosetta," I think it was, in the key of F major.
>
> During that period (am I sounding too much like Dr. Watson? I must have another look at that contract) the closest Dave got to F major was an occasional reluctant B chord.
>
> "Wild," I said as we disbanded. "BAD changes, babe, like tote Wigsville" (or whatever they said in those days).
>
> "White man," replied Dave stonily, "speak with forked tongue." And he left.

The very successful tour brought back all the closeness that had characterized the association of the four performers, especially the once-antagonistic relationship between Paul and Morello. This was underlined by Morello's having to pull out of the last three days because of the rapid failing of what remained of his vision.

It was agreed, however, that the Quartet would get together again, and a tour of Europe was sketched out. This was not to be, for, during a routine medical check-up, it was discovered that Paul had lung cancer. He took chemotherapy and continued to work, taking a less-strenuous tour with the Two Generations of Brubeck, the final concert occurring at Avery Fisher Hall in New York on February 4, 1977. Paul had to have blood a transfusion just to have enough energy to play that night.

Joe Morello, by now pulling through the latest crisis with his eyes, sent Steve Forster, one of his drum students, to stay with Paul and sort of look after him.

There were visitors, including bassist Charles Mingus, long a close friend of both Brubeck and Desmond. Mingus, a massive figure who happened to be dressed all in black (including a cape), stood a long while beside the sleeping figure of his friend. Paul, waking up, saw him as an apparition. He later told Dave, "I thought the Man had come for me!"

Death did come a few days later—Memorial Day, May 30, 1977. Paul Desmond was fifty-three.

Jimmy Lyons, who played such an important part in the early careers of both Dave and Paul, confirmed that he, in carrying out Paul's wishes, flew over San Francisco's Golden Gate and scattered Paul's ashes into the bay. He also drank one last, solemn martini to Paul, with whom he had shared so many over the years.

Paul had long been a part of the extended Brubeck family. He was very close to Dave and Iola's second son, Michael and, in his will, left Michael his alto sax. Darius Brubeck says he was twelve before he learned that Paul was not really his uncle. And, despite that early incident when Desmond's self-absorption left Dave stranded with no job and a wife and two kids to support, Dave now says, "Over the years, he was the most loyal friend I had."

Time for Family

Dave and Iola Brubeck are the parents of six children, the eldest being Darius, born in San Francisco June 14, 1947. He was named for his father's teacher, composer Darius Milhaud. He was followed soon by Michael, Chris, Catherine, Daniel, and Matthew. To no one's surprise, each sibling grew to maturity involved in music, imbued with it so deeply that it was as natural and necessary as breathing.

It didn't follow, in the obligatory sense, that four of the boys should eventually tour with and record with their father. But, to Dave's great delight, that is what happened with Darius on electronic keyboards; Chris, electric bass and trombone; Danny, drums; and Matthew, cello. Each is, as a matter of individual choice, extremely well schooled in the language of music, and each has developed musical tastes that embrace everything from classical to rock, folk to twelve-tone, mainstream to very contemporary jazz, and all the fusions possible between. Given their maternal grandmother's and uncles' notable careers in music, and their father's eclectic interest in *all* things musical, along with his constant reaching toward new horizons, the Brubeck clan is one of the more productive and altogether interesting since the heyday of another notable musical family—that of J. S. Bach.

On any given day at the Brubeck home in Wilton, Connecticut, some combination of Brubecks is almost sure to be busy around the piano in the lower-level music room, which opens onto a green, expansive yard, a stream, a pond, and Dave's composing retreat, a small gazebo on a miniature island across an arched wooden bridge. On a visit during interviews in preparation for this book in May of 1992, Michael and Matthew, the second-oldest and the youngest of the Brubeck brood, had possession of the studio. There were other pianos in other rooms. Dave says, "This house sounded like a conservatory for years and years. In every part of the house, somebody was practicing. Nobody was telling them to practice—in fact sometimes I'd tell them to stop so I could compose!"

Darius, who was already playing piano, started on trumpet at age ten. "I didn't aim at a music career, specifically," he recalls. "I wish I had. I'd be better at a lot of things had I known all along. I studied ethnic musicology and history of religion and had a real liberal arts education, but I didn't do anything about jazz while I was in school, except play it with other students. One thing I did have, and it was sporadic, was training in writing: the ability to just think of things and get them on paper. At a very early age I had lessons in basic music theory."

In fact, according to his father, "His first composition was for four trumpets, and he won the music competition in his school in Oakland. And the teacher said to him, 'Tell your father he wrote a great piece.' I didn't even know he was working on the piece: never heard it or saw it. Think of a kid who's ten years old, and he's really trying to be himself, and that is what the teacher said to him. And that's what my kids have been fighting all their lives.

"They're still fighting it. There was a review of a concert we played in England where everybody had loved us and the critic said, 'How dare these people walk on the same stage with Dave Brubeck!' It's been a long haul for these kids for them to contribute what they have. Everybody thinks, because they're my sons it's been easier. Think again. It's been the opposite."

The teacher's comments in Oakland didn't stop Darius from studying, playing and composing. When he was about fourteen, his uncle, Howard Brubeck, and his father's old friend and musical associate, Bill Smith, guided him further into theory. "I didn't feel pushed, but I think there was a lot of affirmation that I had talent and I had to live up to that," says Darius now. "I think what influenced me a lot, subliminally, were the rehearsals at the house with Dad's quartet. They sounded like fun. It didn't seem like practice. It was four guys together, obviously concentrating on what they were doing but enjoying every moment."

Did Darius play four-hand piano with his dad? "Yeah, sometimes I did, but I always felt intimidated and I think I still do. You know, I'd had some piano in grade school and junior high and some theory; then, one summer in Aspen, when I was fifteen, I got to study composition with Darius Milhaud himself. I wrote some things and, as primitive as they probably were, I got some encouragement from him. So I was serious about writing music but not especially serious about playing until I got into my mid-twenties and realized that I didn't have any other marketable skill."

What Darius didn't say was that he had soon-to-emerge skills as a teacher, first at the Connecticut Center for Continuing Education after his graduation with high honors from Wesleyan University in Middletown, Connecticut, and then as Director of the New Center for Jazz and Popular Music and Associate Professor in Jazz Studies at the University of Natal in Durban, South Africa.

"My wife Cathy is South African, though we met here in the States. In 1982, during a break in my work schedule, Cathy wanted to go home after many years to see her mother, who was very old. So we did go, and I managed to pick up a few gigs there, enough to pay for hotels and food and stuff. One of the people Cathy had introduced me to in New York was the then-head of the music department at the University of Natal. When we got to Durban, I called him up and he said, 'This is really fortuitous. I've just persuaded the university senate to pass, in principle, that the university could have a jazz course and could give degrees to people specializing in jazz on the condition that someone qualified could be found to head that up. How about you?'"

It turned out that the easy part of the job was teaching. The more difficult part was the time that Darius spent "trying to help acclimate underprivileged students who came from no-running-water to where a lot of people were accustomed to using word processors." It was the first program offered by the music department that specifically drew Africans (Black and White) who were beyond school age into the university—people who had left school or whose school had burned down during riots. These students, some of them working musicians, needed theory and overall formal training and were deeply motivated.

By this period in his life, Darius had toured, as keyboardist, with Two Generations of Brubeck (1971 to 1976), recorded for Atlantic records and, subsequently, played concerts and festivals in Europe, South America, all over the United States, and in Africa with the New Brubeck Quartet (Dave, Darius, Chris, and Dan). He had also worked with guitarist Larry Coryell and had his own group, Gathering Forces. Thus he was uniquely qualified and greatly attracted to these aspiring young musicians.

Shortly after Christmas, 1987, Darius brought nine of his students to the United States to the International Association of Jazz Educators gathering in Detroit. Iola and Dave had all of them, plus the other brothers, their sister, and assorted grandchildren in the Wilton house over the holidays. The talk, the noise, the food, and, above all, the music that went on constantly inspired Dave to compose a piece called "Jazzanians" recorded with Chris and Dan and showcasing Dan's ferocious, polyrhythmed drumming in a Music-Masters album called *Trio Brubeck,* released in the summer of 1993.

The youngest of the Brubeck sons, Matthew, was born May 9, 1961. Like his brother and his sister, he started out on piano but later switched his major interest to cello. "I just heard the instrument and liked the sound of it and decided that was what fit my temperament. Probably had I known how complicated it can be to be a cellist, I might not have chosen it. No one really wants a jazz cello player, so you have to make a place for yourself. It's not like being a bass player or drummer where people really need you."

Why did Matthew feel compelled to make music his life's work? "I didn't think there was another way to make a living." He took piano lessons from the time he was eight or nine, and cello lessons started at age twelve. He attended Choate School, and he graduated cum laude from Yale in 1983. This was followed by a master's degree in cello performance from Yale, and he went on to teach at San

Jose State for several years, during which time he also played in a half-dozen area symphony orchestras, created his jazz duo with David Widelock and composed for the Bay Area Jazz Composer's Orchestra. He is currently a member of the Berkeley Symphony.

In 1995, Matthew became a member of the Clubfoot Orchestra, a ten-piece ensemble dedicated to the composition and performance of music written for classic silent films. His initial assignment was to write music for specific scenes for G. W. Pabst's 1929 film, *Pandora's Box*. Other orchestra members created music for other scenes. With Dierdre McClure conducting, the score was premiered in May in San Francisco, as part of the International Film Festival there.

There's a fourteen-year difference between the ages of Darius and Matthew, and by the time Matthew was born, the family had moved to Wilton, and Dave's touring had been greatly curtailed. But for the older boys, missing their Dad was severe and frequent. Darius recalls, "His longest continuous tour was nine months, but it wouldn't be unusual not to see him for two weeks, six weeks, two months, and maybe even longer, and then we'd get to have him for relatively short times. He tried to offset that by sometimes taking us with him to places that would be a base for him. I remember a wonderful summer we spent at the Music Inn near Tanglewood in Lenox, Massachusetts. He was working at the Newport Jazz Festival and other nearby summer gigs at a time when Ornette Coleman was being discovered, and the Modern Jazz Quartet was there along with Gunther Schuller, and I was old enough to understand those experiences. I think things like that more than made up for the emotional problems of absent fatherhood, because when we were with him it was something special."

Unlike Darius, Matthew went away to boarding school (Choate), and by time he was fifteen, his mother was able to actually go on tour with his father, which she had been waiting for many years to do. Darius says, "She was and is, on every level, the anchor and the organizer."

Dave hated the road: he *always* hated the road, but it was the only way he could survive until the Quartet became famous and therefore high priced. The move to Wilton from Oakland made it possible to make short forays nearby or quick trips to Europe. He could be with his kids who were by then moving into their teens. "No teenage time is good," says Dave. "In the late sixties and early seventies, you had some really tough times for teenagers and their families, so I decided I had to be with the kids more. I would go all summer with the kids, camping, for example. One year we went all together on a boat called Campus at Sea and sailed all over the Mediterranean, and for six weeks, I knew where my kids were."

Did the kids manage to totally escape the drug scene? "As much as could be hoped for," responds Dave. "Some kids completely, but I don't know about all the kids. I know they all turned out very well, but I know I don't know everything, and I was afraid of some of their friends. Timothy Leary was holding forth at the universities and got to know Darius, so I don't know the whole story there. But these were things I wanted to be around to counteract."

As for living up to being sons of the celebrated Dave Brubeck, Matthew says, "people expected you to be a carbon copy, especially of his style. Or they might just expect your music to be of a special direction. But there sure were advantages to all this, like name recognition and meeting people. Like, I'd go play someplace with my Dad in Europe and then meet some promoter and then bug them about my own group." One of his own groups, the Lower String Trio, composed of viola, cello, and bass, is interested strictly in new, formal music, not jazz, and Matthew himself has been expanding his horizons by recording with his father and brother Chris in several recent MusicMaster albums. It is generally conceded that he is one of the few cellists capable of playing classical, scored orchestral, and jazz music with equal ability. A fine example is "Looking at a Rainbow" from the *Quiet as the Moon* (1991) release, in which Matthew joins Bobby Militello on flute, Jack Six on bass, and Randy Jones on drums to play Dave's impression of how a rainbow would look from outer space. The lines are long and languid and rather Debussylike. Compare it, then, with the "Forty Days" track from the same collection, in which the cello improvises on a theme from Dave's first oratorio. Matthew swings both in pizzicato and bowed passages. In 1993 he recorded with Darius in South Africa, with South African musicians, on an English label, B & W. These sessions produced two collections of what reviewers called world music, integrating East Indian, jazz, and classical elements and featuring Depak Ram on *bansuri,* an Indian flute. The CDs are called *Gathering Forces I* and *Gathering Forces II.* In 1994, Matthew, with guitarist David Widelock, also recorded a B&W album called *Giraffes in a Hurry.* Compositions here are by Matthew, Widelock, and Thelonius Monk.

All the Brubeck boys share Dave's obvious love of performing, his visceral response to the playing of others, his warm and disarming smile, and (except for Chris, perhaps because of his beard) Dave's very Indian, hawklike features. All are tall, of course (Matthew stands six feet eight inches).

You will note that, from time-to-time, the boys—Christopher, especially—refer to their father simply as "Dave" instead of Dad or Pop or Father.

Chris, born March 19, 1952, is perhaps the most intensely educated son from a musical point of view, having chosen Interlochen Arts Academy in Michigan for his high school. This was a private school which offered extremely demanding music studies. Much earlier, as a fourth grader, he had joined his grade school's band to play trombone and then the Norwalk Youth Symphony and National Music Camp Orchestra. He started his own rock band, New Heavenly Blue, at Interlochen where he played piano and learned to play bass guitar, and was a key member of another group, Sky King. This eclectic young performer spent two years on the road with the folk duo, Addis and Crofut. He then majored on trombone at the University of Michigan before joining Two Generations of Brubeck and the next incarnation, the New Brubeck Quartet.

Of course, every Brubeck child studied piano. Chris remembers, "At one point there was one piano teacher who came to the house and gave five lessons in a row, each one a half-hour. Dave finally got into the bribery system where he'd give each of us a quarter for every time we'd seriously practice for half an hour. We each had our own little cigar boxes in which we kept the quarters we got instead of getting a regular allowance. I remember, when the teacher came, we'd all be, like, playing football. 'Oh no, my turn! I'll be back in a half-hour. Let me come back in and play quarterback!'"

As for choosing the trombone, Chris can't recall being simply handed the instrument and told, "We need a trombone in the band, so this is what you're going to play," but he was interested in band and liked the instrument from the fourth grade on. He also appears to have been especially physically endowed for the instrument. "I remember Dave took me to a concert on Long Island where he was double-billed with Louis Armstrong. Dave introduced me to Louis and said, 'This is my son Chris and he's learning to play trombone.' Now, I have very fat lips. Louis said, 'Oh yeah? You got the chops for it!' That really felt like the pope's blessing, as far as I was concerned."

Chris today plays a bass trombone with an "F-trigger" attachment, designed to permit alternate positions and allow him to do things with facility and speed that an ordinary slide wouldn't permit. His tone is often broad and sometimes rough, evoking the style of New Orleans players such as Kid Ory (of whom Chris never heard), but with ideas all his own. The sound can, on the other hand, be pure and quite romantic. Listen to the "King for a Day" track on the 1993 MusicMaster album, *Trio Brubeck*, for the down-and-dirty Chris, and to the "Over the Rainbow" cut for the soft and singing tone. On the "Rainbow" track, Dave plays the tune in two keys at the same time, and Chris follows through by alternating key centers from phrase to phrase. On paper, it seems a little weird, but as executed, it both teases and pleases the ear. Chris, overdubbing, also plays bass on both tracks.

The playing of the electric bass grew out of playing the guitar, with initial instruction from brother Darius. But Chris has a special view of the qualifications for playing bass, whether it be acoustic (which he has yet to play) or electric (which he very nearly makes sound acoustic). "You have to have the *personality* to be a bass player. Most bass players are 'people persons.' You spend a lot of your time being supportive of other musicians and not that much time in the limelight. You have to be the sort of person who, generally, is into holding the fort, like Eugene Wright did in the old days with Dave. He had both the time to keep and the harmonic thing to keep track of. And, when you're playing with Dave, you've got to be very aware of what his left hand is doing. The more modern piano players will rarely play roots with their left hand; Dave does all the time. You're either with him, or you're conflicting with him. I grew up seeing Gene, knowing he's the guy who plays bass and sort of keeps it together for people. He's not being flashy, he's helping out, and that's the sort of person I am anyhow. If Gene wasn't a musician, he'd be running a YMCA or something, helping kids out."

In the summer of 1993 Chris had rejoined Bill Crofut to play "a jazzy kind of folk," playing trombone, bass, piano, and also singing. Working often with symphony orchestras, he had done all the scoring of their arrangements. Appearances have been with such major groups as the Pittsburgh, Houston, and Cincinnati orchestras. For Cincinnati he also scored tracks for their *Happy Trails* album and arranged a whole concert of Beatles music for them. The concept Chris brought to this project was as far away from elevator music and the Boston Pops as you can get. He grew up loving the Beatles and wanted to bring out what he calls their "soul spirit," using large forces in imaginative ways. It was a great disappointment that the score, although performed in concert, was never recorded.

In 1994, however, there were two recorded adventures of Chris with Bill Crofut. They are called "Unscuare Dance" (which of course includes father Dave's well-known original of that name) and the provocatively-titled "Red, White and Blues." These sessions were released by Albany Records. In early 1995, Chris and Bill were hard at work in the recording studio with opera diva Frederica von Stade. They were preparing a collection of pieces composed by Dave and Chris Brubeck, with lyrics by Chris and his mother, Iola.

As a composer, Chris Brubeck has also co-authored the musical, *David, Champion of Israel;* a musical comedy, *Happy Hanukkah Recklaw;* a choral piece for 260 voices, *Wisdom;* and a concerto for bass trombone and orchestra, commissioned by the Bridgeport Symphony Youth Orchestra. He was the soloist in its premiere performance. He has composed lyrics for a number of his father's pieces and written a great many songs, some of which have been chart hits by such pop artists as Patti LaBelle and Bobby Womack.

Dan Brubeck, born May 4, 1955, never for a moment doubted which instrument would be his choice for a life's work. "As far back as I can remember I wanted to play drums. My Mom says I used to pull pots and pans out in the kitchen and pound on them. Dave's group used to rehearse at the house all the time, so there was always a drum set there, and I had access to them. Of course I was always a great admirer of Joe Morello, and I watched him a lot. I studied with him briefly, but it felt like years because I used to watch him like a hawk."

Dan points how there is a continuum at work. "I see lots of similarities between my playing and Morello's. I arrange my drum solos in the same way he does—how the solo is developed, going from soft to loud and so forth. We're not so much alike, though, in the time-keeping role. In a single rhythm, Morello was a steady time-keeper, mostly with brushes. My forte is polyrhythms, more foreground. A lot of that I got from Joe, even while listening to more modern drummers."

The word "modern" keeps turning up when a Brubeck son compares his style and technique with those of the greats of the recent past. It's deceptive, in that it is not used in any way as a put-down, but essentially means "currently popular."

Danny admired and listened to Morello's successor, Alan Dawson and to Jack De Johnette and Tony Williams. These are all musical drummers, respectful and supportive of the other players but very foreground, not simply a modest part of the rhythm section.

Dan was formally trained in music, spending a summer at Berklee School of Music (studying with Alan Dawson) and getting the full treatment in theory and harmony at the Interlochen Arts Academy and the North Carolina School of the Arts. All through this, by the way, he was playing one of Joe Morello's old drum sets, later switching to a more contemporary set.

The first professional gig for Dan Brubeck was with brothers Darius and Chris for a summer in a rock-jazz group, the New Bag. He appeared with his father and brother Chris (playing bass) with the Alaska Symphony and the Honolulu Symphony in the jazz segments of Dave's *The Light in the Wilderness,* when he was in his early teens. At seventeen, he joined Two Generations of Brubeck, and was the drummer with the New Brubeck Quartet from 1977 to 1979, recording with his family and performing with Gerry Mulligan, Paul Desmond, Jon Hendricks, and many others. His love of rock never flagged, but it fused well with jazz and reached a peak, in terms of success, with the Dolphins, whose complex fusion recordings held on the radio play charts for some time.

The Dolphins have been remarkably successful in serving as a bridge between the "Old World" and the "New World." They like to say that they are "augmenting, not just repeating" traditions. Mostly, their music is easy on the uneducated ear. With Mike DeMicco on electric guitar, Rob Leon on bass, Vinnie Martucci playing keyboards, and Dan Brubeck on drums, their sometimes psychedelic performances can also take on old standards like "Caravan" and add new twists to "Blue Rondo a la Turk."

Darius, Chris, and Dan were all part of Two Generations of Brubeck, which started in 1972. At that time Darius had his own group, the Darius Brubeck Ensemble; Dave had a trio with Alan Dawson and Jack Six; and Chris had his rock group, New Heavenly Blue and later Sky King. Iola Brubeck says, "They'd do a show that would present each of the groups, and they'd end with an ensemble with everybody. A favorite was 'Blue Rondo,' and there was a terrific blues harmonica player with the rock group by the name of Peter 'Madcat' Ruth who, to a kind of shuffle rhythm, added something 'Blue Rondo' had never had before."

Two Generations of Brubeck traveled and concertized in Australia, New Zealand, Mexico, Canada, Germany, Austria, Holland, Switzerland, and, of course, all over the United States. They recorded often for Atlantic, sometimes with Perry Robinson (son of composer Earl Robinson) on clarinet, Jerry Bergonzi on soprano and tenor sax, and Randy Powell, percussion.

All this talent, of diverse tastes and techniques, became impractical when it came time for a European tour where jazz and only jazz was to be played. Jazz promoter George Wein asked Dave to take only the family members and to call the group the New Brubeck Quartet, and so it became from 1977 to 1979. Darius played synthesizer and electric keyboard, Chris was playing both electric bass and bass trombone, and Danny was on percussion.

During all this family touring, the performers were inevitably and insistently asked to do all the old favorites, from "Take Five" and "Blue Rondo a la Turk" to "The Duke," and "Some Day My Prince Will Come." Danny says that his approach to playing these so-well-remembered chestnuts was to never do anything verbatim but to remember some of the approaches taken by Joe Morello in the original and to use some of those approaches—in other words, not the original taste but the same general flavor. It seemed to work. Long-time Quartet fans were not offended, and new and younger listeners became new supporters. Through it all, of course, Dave was the dominant factor, continuing on in his "Own Sweet Way."

Chris Brubeck remembers, "One of the most extreme reactions we got was on our first tour of Europe with the New Brubeck

Quartet. We went to Germany. One night the promoter came backstage, and he was just very emotional with what was going on with German audiences. Apparently, on top of reacting to what we were doing musically, there was this magical thing for them of a father playing with his kids—despite the fact that we kids were skinny and had long hair and looked like hippies. A few people reacted badly to that; they didn't like us at all. But the promoter said that far more liked it than not, partly because the German kids *really* had a generation gap with their parents. They'd look back at World War II and say, 'Boy, did you really screw that up! Not only do *I* have that distance from you as a teenager but the whole world does, too, because you were involved in that Hitler thing.' It was the bridging of the gap that seemed to reach both the fathers and sons in the audience."

Neither of the two other Brubeck siblings was destined to play professionally—Michael because of a learning disability caused at birth and Catherine, who was born November 5, 1953, chose marriage and a career as wife and mother. Dave points out that "she has many talents. Cathy played flute and piano. In fact, she was very musical. In my estimation, she is as musical as any of the boys, but the boys kind of scared her off. She had, I think, an innate talent to be an actress and also a painter and also a musician, but for some reason, she didn't want to ever pursue it professionally. She married an Armenian, Arnold Yaghsizian, and they live near us, and they have three children. 'Elana Joy' is the title of one of my compositions and was named for their first child, a daughter. Now they have a two-year-old boy, and I've written a piece for him, an Armenian dance. His name is Daniel Arnold Charis Yaghsizian." A daughter, Mariel Grace, was born in early 1995.

Cathy is a graduate of Sarah Lawrence College. She says her interest in music was "just average" and adds, "It was hard to be average around Dave, Darius, Chris, Dan, and Matthew." She studied piano and then, for many years, flute and dance, especially ballet. She also demonstrated talent in the pictorial arts. It was only natural that Cathy should wind up at Interlochen Arts Academy in Michigan, along with brother Dan (Chris had gone before).

Today, all of Cathy's training has left its mark, but her primary role is that of wife and mother. She and her husband, Arnold, run a housecleaning business from their Connecticut home. "When I have time," she says, "I have a big, thick file of children's stories I've written. I have one that's really 100 percent finished, and I'm really happy with it. I'm going to make a try at getting it published. But I have maybe fifty more. Some start as I make up bedtime tales for my kids, and, while they're falling asleep, I'll rush downstairs to jot them down and go from there."

American history is of great interest to Cathy, and she notes that, these days, very few "character-building" stories containing historical figures are written for very young children. So she, for example, has written a story about Indians and the first Thanksgiving. She says, "I have a feeling it's going to be terribly *non*-politically correct, since I'm doing it as a 'friendly' thing, and everybody hates Thanksgiving now: all you get is the 'White-guilt' rap."

Cathy says that she had a born-again religious experience at age nineteen and has since been a Bible student, in a nondenominational way. "My father and I have a lot of fun trading books back and forth," she says. "He's been my major influence in that area."

Cathy met her husband at a Bible-study class. Arnold, says Cathy, is not musical, but their young son may carry on the Brubeck tradition. Daniel Arnold has, says his mother, a definite bent toward sounds and loves everything that appeals to the ear.

Second son Michael is very special to his family, as they are to him.

ONCE WHEN I WAS VERY YOUNG

Once when I was very young, with a twinkling
   in my eye,
I looked at life with a curious view, as the days
   rolled slowly by.
I listened with the ear of a child to the sounds
   of birds in flight,
And shivered 'neath my covers when the dark
   snuffed out the light.
But in the lazy days of summer, when the
   daylight lingered on,
We played our games of hide-and-seek and
   daydreamed on the lawn.
The summer nights were spent with friends, when
   we tried with all our might

To fight away the webs of sleep and wait for
   dawn's first light.
These golden days are long past now. I've grown
   into a man.
But the memories of childhood I still hold in my
   hand.
I've given up the things of youth, like toys
   and dolls and trains
And traded them for others, like work and aches
   and pains.
But in my mind I wonder if I could go back still
And live those days of misspent youth on
   summer's peaceful hills.
Once when I was so very young with a twinkling
   in my eye,
I looked at life with a curious view as the days
   rolled slowly by.

Poem by Michael Brubeck, edited by John Jenney.

What might have been a tragedy for the family ultimately became a triumph and a test of faith. When Michael was born on March 18, 1949, doctors found that he was suffering from an unidentified rash and signs of jaundice.

Dave says, "They just took Michael away from us and put him in isolation. In hindsight, we know that he must have been fighting the incompatibility of his blood type (Rh positive) with his mother's (Rh negative). Not much was known about the Rh factor in those days. Nowadays an ordinary blood transfusion would be performed."

Whether it was the Rh factor trauma that later caused severe learning disabilities is not known. Michael did come home from the hospital an apparently normal, healthy baby, thriving and growing strong and alert, surrounded by love and attention. But in a few years, uneven development involving a poor sense of time and space became apparent. This only partially-understood disability began to interfere with the activities that interested him most.

"His love of music and understanding of other people's music is great," explains Dave. "He and Paul Desmond were very close, and Paul willed Mike his horn, which he treasures. When Iola took him to buy his own horn, when he was just a little kid, when he saw the saxophone he started to cry in anticipation."

In California, Michael began saxophone study and made good progress despite the disability. Then the family moved east to Connecticut. "The new teacher had no sympathy for him and treated him in a way that made him feel he wasn't capable of learning," says Dave. "I know he was, given the right approach. But it seems like everything Mike tried, he ran into stone walls because of his learning disabilities. He also has a very literary mind, which he doesn't devote much time to anymore. But he and Paul used to have great conversations about the latest books.

"His IQ was very high in the testing done *before* he went to school. In our family, the kids are all very bright, and he was maybe the brightest, pre-school." But formal schooling magnified the handicaps, and the barricade of the learning disorder, coupled with stuttering, caused Michael to withdraw more and more. That was not true at home where his sister and all his brothers treated him no differently, with no less affection, than anyone else in the family. So did Paul Desmond, Eugene Wright, and Joe Morello. In fact, says Dave, Michael still remembers everything about the pieces the Quartet played, so close was he to the performers and the constant rehearsals at home. He used to practice sometimes on Joe's drums. And Michael, along with his mother and older brother, accompanied the Quartet to Europe and behind the Iron Curtain in 1958.

He had difficulties in high school, but when Michael graduated, he received an award for his literary work, and one of his poems was published in a national poetry magazine. He tried college, but found the academic work too defeating.

Now in his forties, Michael has an advocate living with him in a separate house, not far from his parents. Companion George Moore chose the term *advocate* to denote his most important function—assisting Michael in dealing with such things as bills, insurance forms, and the challenges of daily living. Moore is a trained therapist who said in the late summer of 1993 that Michael's quality of life is constantly and dramatically improving with the aid of a new medication. Michael spends his mornings riding and caring for his horses at a nearby stable. Evenings often find him visiting friends, and he is in and out of his parents' house frequently. Dave says, "Things are coming along the best they have in years, and he's much happier now."

Michael was particularly pleased by the critical reaction to his poem "Once When I Was Very Young," which began as part of a small book of poems that he gave to his parents one Christmas. Dave later wrote music to fit the text and, in the MusicMasters album bearing the poem's title, it is heard both as a duo for Dave and clarinetist Bill Smith, and as a choral piece by the Gregg Smith Singers. Michael was a beaming participant in September 1992 at the fiftieth wedding anniversary party for Dave and Iola as his words were sung again, this time by members of the extended family.

George Moore is very much a part of the Wilton menage, not just as companion, therapist, and advocate for Michael, but as archivist for the boxes and boxes of memorabilia: programs, itineraries, reviews, clippings, and other papers that have accumulated over the years. At one time he also managed Danny's band, the Dolphins. In 1994, when the Brubecks' office manager, Juliet Gerlin, retired, George added her duties to everything else. A year later, he was still discovering how totally involved she had been, both as the gateway to Dave and Iola for all outsiders and as the only person who knew about all pending activities and how to keep them on course.

*Dave Brubeck and
Louis Armstrong at
a New York City
recording session for
The Real Ambassadors
in September 1961.*

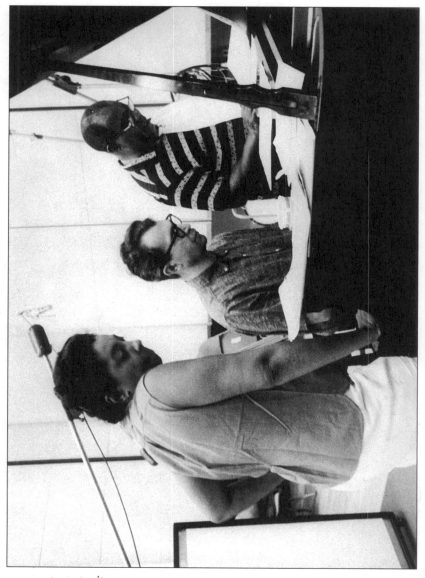

Carmen McRae, Dave Brubeck, and Louis Armstrong, at a rehearsal for the recording of The Real Ambassadors, September 1961.

*A formal portrait of Dave and
Paul Desmond, circa 1962.*

The Brubeck family in Wilton, Connecticut, 1963. LEFT TO RIGHT: Iola, Matthew, Catherine, Dave, Danny, Chris, Michael, and Darius.

The Classic Quartet plays the Johnson White House in 1964. The occasion is a dinner concert during a visit by King Hussein of Jordan.

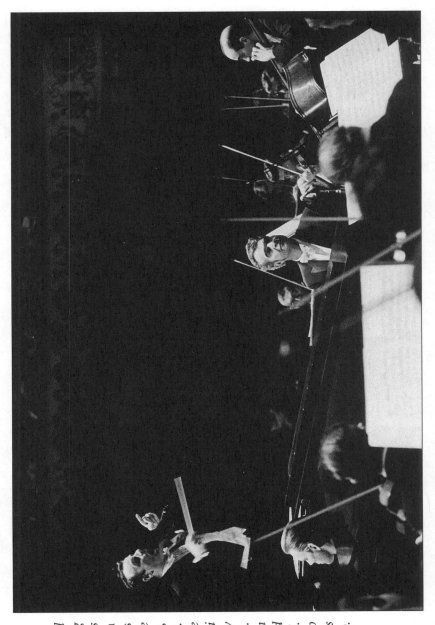

Erich Kunzel conducting Dave Brubeck's The Light in the Wilderness in its premiere performance, February 1968. He leads the Cincinnati Symphony Orchestra. Baritone William Justus is seated just below Kunzel. The bassist to Brubeck's left is Frank Proto.

Dave and Gerry Mulligan.

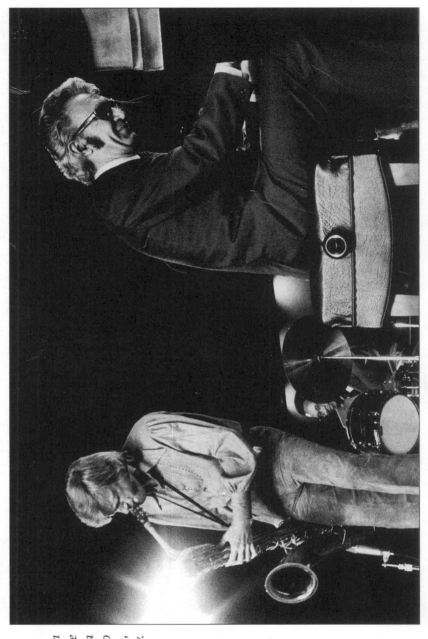

Gerry Mulligan and Dave Brubeck at a concert in 1970 in Berlin, Germany.

*Paul Desmond, Dave Brubeck,
Gerry Mulligan, Alan Dawson,
and Jack Six with the Boston
Pops Orchestra in the early
1970s, Symphony Hall, Boston.*

Gerry Mulligan, Alan Dawson, and Dave Brubeck at a concert in the early 1970s.

*Chris Brubeck,
Perry Robinson,
Jerry Bergonzi,
Pete "Madcat" Ruth,
on stage, 1973—
one configuration of
Two Generations
of Brubeck.*

Two Generations of Brubeck: Dave Brubeck and sons, Chris, Dan, and Darius. (Photograph courtesy of Sutton Artists Corporation.)

*The Dave Brubeck Quartet with
Butch Miles, Jerry Bergonzi, Chris
Brubeck, and Dave Brubeck.*
(Photograph courtesy of Sutton
Artists Corporation.)

Butch Miles, drums; Chris Brubeck, electric bass; Dave Brubeck, piano; and Jerry Bergonzi, sax, probably at the Concord Jazz Festival, 1979.

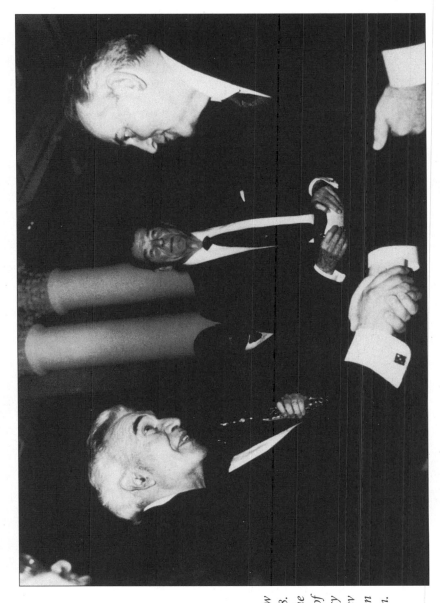

The Moscow Summit in 1988. Dave receives the congratulations of General Secretary Mikhail Gorbachev as Ronald Reagan looks on.

← *Clarinetist Bill Smith with Darius Brubeck at piano during Dave and Iola's fiftieth anniversary party at the Claremont Hotel in Oakland, California, 1992.*

↙ *Gerry Mulligan, Norman Bates, and Danny Brubeck at the fiftieth wedding anniversary celebration.*

↓ *Bill Smith, Gerry Mulligan, and Chris Brubeck at all-night jam session at Dave and Iola's fiftieth wedding anniversary celebration.*
(Photographs by the author.)

*The Dave Brubeck Quartet
with Jack Six, Randy Jones,
Dave Brubeck, and Bill Smith,
1992.* (Photograph courtesy of
Sutton Artists Corporation.)

Dave on the deck of the gazebo at the "Wilton Hilton," the Brubeck family home in Wilton, Connecticut, 1993. (Photograph by the author.)

Lower level of the Brubeck home in Wilton, Connecticut, 1993. (Photograph by the author.)

Dave Brubeck standing at the combination keyboard and easel in the gazebo in his backyard, 1993. (Photograph by the author.)

Darius at the piano and Matthew with his cello in the music room of the Brubeck home, 1993. (Photograph by the author.)

Iola and Dave Brubeck, 1993.
(Photograph by the author.)

The Dave Brubeck Quartet, 1993: Randy Jones, Dave Brubeck, Bill Smith, and Jack Six. (Photograph courtesy of Sutton Artists Corporation.)

President Bill Clinton, presenting Dave with the National Medal of the Arts at the White House, October 14, 1994. Actress Julie Harris, another honoree, is in the background.

Dave, wearing the National Medal of
Arts, and Iola outside the White House.

Time for
Compatriots: II

The Classic Quartet and all that followed, including the celebrated and amazingly successful "Time" albums as well as Dave's equally successful "serious" music career, would have remained unborn and unheard without those who worked with Brubeck in the scuffling early years. Musicians like Dave Van Kriedt (tenor), Bill Smith (clarinet), Dick Collins (trumpet), Bob Collins (trombone), Jack Weeks (bass), and Cal Tjader (drums) were the nucleus of the early Octet. Other fine performers in Dave's formative career include bassists Ron Crotty, Wyatt "Bull" Ruther, Norman and Bob Bates, and Joe Benjamin as well as long-time friends, drummers Joe Dodge and Lloyd Davis.

It's interesting that the early success of the Dave Brubeck Quartet came with almost no outside professional help except for the championing of the group by Jimmy Lyons, later the major force behind the Monterey Jazz Festival, then an important San Francisco radio personality.

Iola says that she would write the bios and try to make publicity contacts, but there wasn't really any genuine publicity until Brubeck signed with Columbia and Debbie Ishlon took over. She's the one who probably got Brubeck the cover of *Time*, Iola says. She adds that Brubeck not only didn't have a publicity agent, but also had no personal management until Mort Lewis took that job in about 1956. Lewis was a strong manager for a few years—until his departure to manage the Brothers Four and, eventually, Simon and Garfunkel. Then it was Brubeck and Iola who once again did double and triple duty until Russell Gloyd came aboard.

The success of the Quartet obviously was not hype, although plenty of that came along as the years moved on. Dave is shy but not modest, nor should he be. There is plenty about which to boast, especially concerning the period that began with the Classic Quartet with Brubeck, Desmond, Wright, and Morello.

The joy of making music has continued in all of the later incarnations of the Brubeck Quartet. It is still evident in the performances of the group that worked on recordings and concerts in the eighties and nineties: Dave, Bill Smith, bassist Jack Six, and drummer Randy Jones.

Born in England, Randy Jones, like Dave, is self-taught, listening to records, playing with friends. At sixteen he, like the Beatles, went to Germany to play mostly rhythm and blues in clubs around Hamburg. R&B is what he played at work, but he had fallen in love with bebop several years before, listening to the recordings of Max Roach, Miles Davis, and Philly Joe Jones. Bop is what he practiced whenever he could.

His ambitions to play jazz were shelved for awhile when a Las Vegas-based group of Nisei, called Takeuchi Keigo and his Imperial Japanese Dancers, toured Europe, heard Jones, and invited him to be their music director. He was only eighteen. "We played mostly hotels, especially the Hilton chain—the Hong Kong Hilton, the Cairo Hilton. I learned to read music on my own when we rehearsed shows," says Randy. "It turned out I was pretty good at it."

By the time Jones was twenty-two or twenty-three, he was working in England as a studio musician. "There wasn't any real jazz playing to do. I was with the BBC group of other young freelancers and got to work with touring American stars like Tony Bennett when they did concerts or recordings in England." It was in England that Maynard Ferguson found him in 1967, and he became a member of Ferguson's hard-blowing big band for six years. In the United States, he worked casuals with Chet Baker, Gerry Mulligan, and others and toured awhile with Harry James. By 1978, Jones was asked to join the Brubeck Quartet for a summer tour while regular drummer, Butch Miles, took another temporary gig. A few months later Jones replaced Miles permanently.

One of Brubeck's remarkable traits is his acceptance and nourishment of players from many schools, even while he continues to develop his own clearly-defined style. Bop had a lock on many of the younger players, and Dave has worked successfully with lots of them, including his own children. Chris Brubeck was playing electric bass with the Quartet when Randy Jones came aboard. Chris doubled on trombone, while Jerry Bergonzi played tenor sax and doubled on electric bass for Chris.

These musicians represented a radical switch from the Classic Quartet of Joe Morello, Gene Wright, and Paul Desmond, who had been swinging all through the heyday of bebop. How did Randy Jones adapt to the drum chair that Morello had defined for so long? "Dave never really imposed any of that on me," says Jones. "I never thought about it much, but certainly playing in odd time signatures was a challenge. The first time we played 'Take Five,' Dave said, 'How do you feel about soloing in five?' I said, 'I have no idea.'" But it all worked out. "Jerry Bergonzi was there playing tenor, and he really liked my bop-influenced playing. It sure was a different group than it had been, though!"

Jones has noticed some changes in the way Brubeck approaches concertizing, especially since his lingering influenza related illness of 1992–93. He has reduced his schedule and, says Randy, "His set-calling, the choosing of tunes in sequence, has been unusually precise. There were years when he would call sets and then play wholly different things. Of course, he can still fool you. Sometimes he'll play introductions, and we're all looking at each other and talking out of the sides of our mouths, saying, 'What the hell is *this* going to be?'"

Neither Jones nor bassist Jack Six contributes complete originals to the Quartet's repertoire, but both play a part in the composition process, as do the horn soloists (most often Bill Smith). Six says, "Dave writes the tune, with maybe a conceptual idea. I may add a bass line, and everybody contributes to what the audience eventually hears."

Six is a veteran player, schooled in composition at Julliard, seasoned by years in navy bands, where he was leader and trumpet player, later switching to acoustic bass. He played with the Tommy Dorsey ghost band under Warren Covington, played with Woody Herman, and was musical director for the Claridge Hotel and Casino in Atlantic City from its opening in 1981 to 1985.

Jack had, however, been working with Dave Brubeck much of the time since 1968, when he was a member of the Quartet that made Dave's third tour of Mexico. Six concentrated on studio work around New York during the "Two Generations of Brubecks" years and for some time after, while Chris Brubeck continued as bassist for the Quartet. But by 1990, Jack was, except for occasional "family specials," again the full-time bassist.

Six says the years with Brubeck have been "The greatest thing that ever happened to my life—the most important thing I've ever done. I love Dave and Iola and the kids. I've seen them grow up. They're like family to me."

Randy Jones echoes these sentiments. "Fifteen years is a long time; I've enjoyed most of it. The negative things are only logistics. Sometimes you're just really tired; sometimes you get to a place and things haven't been well worked out. But musically and personally it couldn't have been better. And Dave and Iola's kids are great. I've especially enjoyed working with Danny, who ought to move to New York City for better opportunities, and Chris. Chris has such a great spirit—he's always up. He's also a natural mediator."

The current Brubeck compatriot with the most seniority is Bill Smith, who was born not far from Dave's home town, Concord, in Sacramento, California. Bill grew up in the Bay Area and met Dave at Mills College right after the war. Bill had become a clarinetist, he says, "when a door-to-door traveling salesman came around and told my mother that, if I signed up for thirty-two lessons, I'd get a clarinet free. Well, Benny Goodman was already my hero. I jumped at the chance. I was playing with the Oakland Symphony when I was fifteen."

Smith traveled with a regional big band for a year, saved enough money to go to Julliard, and arrived at Mills in 1946 as a graduate student (he was exempted from the war because of a hernia). He says, "Dave and I were both serious about learning what jazz, in the European tradition, held for us. We both had a penchant for exploring, especially counterpoint." The classes of Darius Milhaud and the coming-together of the Octet allowed free reign for experimentation. Although the Octet is now historically famous, it was essentially a rehearsal band. It was, says Bill, "too small for a concert hall, too big for a club."

The Octet did record considerably, as noted elsewhere in this book, and listeners comparing Bill Smith's clarinet playing then with what he is doing with the Brubeck Quartet forty-five years later will notice quite a difference in tone and conception. The first major influence was clearly Goodman, followed by Artie Shaw, whom Smith greatly admired. Then Bill (like Randy Jones), fell under the spell of bebop and wanted to follow in the footsteps of Charlie Parker. Bop didn't captivate Dave as it did Smith, but as Bill says of Brubeck, "I think his playing now sums up his life. Bebop is part of his language, but not its natural habitat. He has an orchestral approach to the piano, sometimes wanting it to sound like a full orchestra, sometimes a reed section, sometimes a brass section. He still has a lot of Art Tatum in him."

Smith won a series of endowments that enabled him to study in Paris and Rome. In 1960, Brubeck came through Rome on a tour, got together with Smith, and put him under contract to conceive and do one album a year with Dave. The first project was *The Riddle*. Then came such memorable Fantasy releases as *Brubeck a la Mode* and *A Near Myth*. *Swinging on a Golden Gate* and a collection called *Witches Bru* were recorded by Columbia, but as of this writing, had never been released. It was rediscovered during research for the four-CD Columbia box-set Brubeck retrospective. (Oddly enough, the title of the next Miles Davis album to be released by Columbia after Dave's recording of *Witches Bru* was called *Bitches Brew*.) Smith says, "These projects were a wonderful example of Dave's generosity. He let me be the leader for those sessions. What I wanted, he obliged me with."

Bill Smith went on to teach and become Director of Contemporary Music at the University of Washington. From 1966 on, he played only occasionally with the Quartet. Then, in 1980, Dave asked him to become a regular. "OK," said Smith, "as long as I can continue to teach at Washington." Brubeck agreed, the university agreed, and that's what Bill Smith has done, as of this writing, ever since.

Here's how Bill Smith sums up Dave Brubeck: "He accepted success gracefully, didn't become arrogant, overbearing, or, like some others, bitter. He stayed the same person, much as he was when he was a student: thoughtful, sensitive, and generous. To me, working with Dave today is about the same as when we were having jam sessions at Mills College. Playing is like having a conversation. Dave is my favorite conversationalist. So, when we have conversations together, we enjoy it a lot, just as we did nearly fifty years ago."

One of the most recent Brubeck additions is Bobby Militello, who plays flute and saxophone. Militello had to replace Bill Smith on a moment's notice in 1981 when Bill was rushed to a hospital with meningitis.

Today, Brubeck's compatriots don't have as much opportunity to rehearse as they had in the old days. An exception may occur for a record date or when, as in October of 1993, Dave brought in a whole batch of new compositions for a week's engagement at the Blue Note in Manhattan. Mostly, however, the group members meet at the location of the first engagement on a tour and rehearse as they travel. An example of a current tour is shown by the itinerary for the summer and fall of 1993:

June 18:	The Sheldon Theater, St. Louis, Missouri.
June 19:	The Wildwood Park Theater, Little Rock, Arkansas.
June 24:	Capitol Theater Festival, Quebec City, Quebec.
June 27:	The Nautical Outdoor Stage, Cleveland, Ohio.
July 9:	Montreal International Jazz Festival, Pelletier Theater, Montreal, Quebec. [with Chris and Dan Brubeck and Bobby Militello as well as the Gerry Mulligan Quartet].
July 15:	Baie Comeau, Quebec.
July 24:	Wilson School Auditorium, Bozeman, Montana.
July 29:	Tower Theater, Fresno, California.
July 31:	Robert Mondavi Winery, Oakville, California.
August 1:	Montalvo, Saratoga, California.
August 20:	Outdoor Band Shell, Kemper Center, Kenosha, Wisconsin.
August 21:	Planting Fields Arboretum, Oyster Bay, Long Island, New York.
September 1:	Hollywood Bowl, Los Angeles [with Lincoln Center Orchestra and other jazz artists].
September 4:	The Lawn of the Grand Hotel, Mackinac Island, Michigan.

September 5:   Ponchartrain Hotel, Detroit, Michigan.
October 5–10:   The Blue Note, New York City.

Dave started this tour still suffering from the effects of his autumn 1992 influenza and the heart-irregularity problems suffered during the winter in Europe, but he began to regain his strength and endurance as the performances continued. It's worth noting, however, that the stress was nothing like it was during the tours of 1958 to 1969, which often required two concerts a day.

Among Dave's compatriots over the years are musicians who have settled nearby, especially Gerry Mulligan. In the early 1950s, Dave worked at the Blackhawk in San Francisco, and Gerry worked at the Haig in Los Angeles, and they would exchange locations— fellow musical pioneers, passing in the night. Both had, of course, heard and admired each other. Dave remembers that he did a concert at Stockton High School at which both groups appeared but played separately. Mulligan and Paul Desmond were also friends. In later years, whenever any or all of these musicians were playing the same gig, they would manage to join together in a grand finale. That was still true at the Montreal International Jazz Festival in July of 1993.

Chris Brubeck has glowing memories of the Montreal Festival. "Gerry Mulligan joined us for a very rousing version of 'Blue Rondo a la Turk' and then we played 'Take Five,' and we really took it in a wild new direction, and after his solo, Gerry came back and said, 'Where have you guys been all my life?' We went into this 5/4 kind of funky New Orleans, sort of second line kind of thing we'd never explored before. It was one of those things that was *searing*, where everyone was exploring and went in the right direction."

Mulligan was impressed by Dave's playing, early on. "He always plays percussively and orchestrally. He gets top marks as both a musician and a human being. Dave has always been a close friend, and from the very start, I've always thought there was a relationship there that probably started in a previous life."

Any musical group requires competent and endless personal, organizational, and logistical support, and Brubeck has been fortunate in this area. Over the years he has developed a support staff that makes his life as a professional performer as easy as it is ever going to be. We come now to three people, in addition to George Moore (whom we've already discussed), who form the core of Dave's managerial and support staff. They are Russell Gloyd, Frank Modica, and Richard Jeweler.

Gloyd, the Brubecks' manager, conductor, and producer is currently headquartered halfway across the continent in Chicago. Dave and Russell first met in 1975 when Dave came to Texas to appear with the Dallas Symphony, for which Russell was the manager of operations. Assigned to Dave, Russell soon found that they worked well and easily together. When Dave returned to Dallas the next year, Russell had just quit the orchestra and was considering other jobs when Dave suggested that he come to work with him.

Dave and Iola had been without personal management for some time; doing it all themselves was becoming more and more time-consuming. Russell joined the team with limited duties that quickly expanded, as did Dave's activities with orchestras and choruses around the world. Soon Russell was conducting at virtually all these events, putting together self-taught skills, early encouragement from his professional-musician mother, some training at North Texas University, some work with conductor-coach Sam Krachmalnick in Los Angeles, and his years as a member of the United States Army Band.

Brubeck's participation in "classical" concert situations is more than just that of composer. His appearance at dress rehearsal has a galvanizing effect on players and singers who only then realize that every Brubeck composition is a work in progress. He is at the keyboard, usually with his Quartet, for those jazz elements in every work that a formal orchestra simply cannot provide. But much preparation must be done prior to Dave's appearance.

Here's how Russell Gloyd describes a typical situation: "In Minneapolis, we did *Gates of Justice* in Orchestra Hall in April [1993]. It was three choirs—rank amateur choirs who had never worked together until my first rehearsal. I had to work very hard in uniting them and bringing off what turned out to be a great performance. It was harder than you can imagine and was done in four rehearsals. As for the orchestra, we did two works. One was the *Pange Lingua Variations* [Russell had conducted the premiere performance in Sacramento], for which I needed an orchestra of about twenty-seven and for *Gates of Justice* an orchestra of about seventeen. These were all the top musicians in the Minneapolis area, so there was no problem there.

"What I try to do as a conductor is raise the level of the performing forces to a point at which Dave can continue to compose his piece. I tell everyone, especially college kids, 'You're beginning your career. You're going to work with the masters, you'll be performing works that go back centuries, you'll be performing new compositions. I'll guarantee you, you'll never have the experience of having the composer on the stage, still composing his piece, which is what improvisation is all about.'"

As Dave's producer, Russell, working on an entirely different level, has to negotiate with assorted record companies, choose music to be included, doctor defective tapes, remix multitrack material, hire additional musicians where needed, see to scores and timings when the music is for a television show, deal with the engineers in the recording studio and thereafter, fight for release dates, and be sure publicity is adequate. Here Peter Levinson Communications is often contracted. Levinson has been working with and for Dave for many years and probably has better contacts within the entertainment industry than anyone.

The fifty-eight selections included in Columbia box collection, *Dave Brubeck: Time Signatures: A Career Retrospective,* is a case in point. It began with lunch in New York in 1991 with Columbia executives who wanted to do a multi-CD release of a long-ago Quartet live performance in Santa Barbara. Russell's opinion was that the tape was OK, but that the studio recordings of the same selections were better. He suggested, instead, "Let's not waste the CD-box idea on this material. Let's just go for the full, definitive collection. Columbia started off wanting to tape just the Columbia material, but I insisted we go for everything."

This meant negotiations with Fantasy, Dave's first recording affiliation, Atlantic, Concord, Russian television, and MusicMasters, covering a period of forty-five years, 1946 to May of 1991. Since, at Columbia alone, there were dozens, maybe hundreds of unreleased recordings (including multitakes, whole sessions, and on-location recordings from all over the world), the next step was for Dave and Russell to go through mountains of material, some of which Dave hadn't heard in years, some of which he had totally forgotten. These had been stored in Columbia's underground storage facilities in their "Iron Mountain."

Dave says, "They leaned on a door [at Iron Mountain] a few months ago, that they didn't know was a door, and it opened into a storage room that nobody had been in for twenty years. They went by it every day—didn't know it was a door! They have a room full of stuff, floor to ceiling, ten boxes high, filling the entire room. I said to Russell, while we were in an elevator, 'Would it fill an elevator?' And he said, 'Six elevators!' I'm running across things I never dreamt I recorded, and some of them are better than other things released."

Not many of these made it (after weeks of listening and relistening) into the four-CD boxed set, but some are turning up in other CD collections as Columbia continues to mine the Brubeck treasures. For example, when *Dave Digs Disney* was transferred to CD, two additional tracks, "Very Good Advice" and "So This Is Love," were included. These had been left out of the original LP release because there wasn't enough room. Five new tracks are to be found in the 1994 re-release of *The Real Ambassadors.* These are by the Quartet, Louis Armstrong, and Carmen McRae.

Once the selection for the boxed set was made, Dave was interviewed by Howard Mandel for the song-by-song commentary in the fat book that goes with the collection, and Doug Ramsey began writing the encapsulated history of Dave Brubeck, also an invaluable part of the release. There was an additional end-of-book interview with Juul Athonissen, director of the Academy of Fine Arts in Belgium. Iola and Juliet Gerlin began digging for photographs.

At the same time, Russell Gloyd, working with Amy Herot and several engineers, began to clean up old tape, which was processed through a new and somewhat tricky electronic system and digitally converted. This processing resulted in unexpected delays, and by the time all the art work had been done and actual production was accomplished, it was late 1992 or early 1993 when the CDs really reached the record stores. That's two years of preproduction and production time.

Another function Russell fulfills is the setting-up of concert tours, whether with the Quartet or other ensembles. The two Russian adventures, one a three-city, fifteen-concert, three-week affair (detailed in chapter 7) and the other an historic performance at the Moscow Summit (see chapter 12) were among them. The logistics were staggering.

Performance scheduling comprises another key element in the Brubeck support equation. Starting in the mid-1950s, Joe Glaser of Associated Booking handled bookings for Dave. Glaser represented Louis Armstrong, Billie Holiday, and many other world-class jazz stars. Dave switched to Larry Bennett around 1968, and Frank Modica of Sutton Artists has scheduled engagements for Dave since 1971. Modica plays an important role in Dave's day-to-day life as a performing artist by lining up dates, sometimes more than a year ahead of time. He negotiates terms, organizes coherent tours all over the United States, and coordinates with a European firm on appearances overseas.

Modica is a veteran both of the big band days and of MCA, having handled bookings for the Dorsey brothers, Charlie Barnet, Harry James, and countless other musicians of that time when being on the road was a way of life. He laments that things have changed radically in the past few years. "It's tough; you have to be careful because nobody has any money. Symphony orchestras are going bankrupt all over the country. Colleges and universities and everyone have a cash-flow problem. But Dave is a known commodity. He still gets his price and as many bookings as he wants. Dave's in a different stratum. I don't have to deal with fly-by-night promoters. What I *do* have to put up with is bureaucrats, many of whom don't have a clue as to what they're doing. Remember all the big theaters that had live acts? They're called 'performing-arts centers' now, and they book in wholesale lots a year or two years in advance. We're no longer dealing with professional people who grew up in the music business. We're dealing with people who are in the *marketing* business."

Modica coordinates bookings with Russell Gloyd, who has the task of getting musicians together and arranging for transportation and accommodations and the many other essentials of a successful tour. And Frank Modica is very concerned with the time of year and the weather when making bookings. "Dave says, 'If it's a gig in January or February, be careful where you book me.' In other words, if it's Marquette, Michigan, forget about it until it's spring—who needs the snow and ice and getting stuck, and they've got to dig you out to get to the next job!" This concern presents a marked contrast to the struggling days when Dave would have to take just about any gig he could get anywhere, any time, and be there in any weather fair or foul.

"I've been through all kinds of performers," says Modica. "Dave's one of the sweetest, nicest men I've ever met. He's not egotistical. He's understanding, and he listens to me."

And at seventy-four, Dave remained a client with an emotional need to work. By 1993, Modica was trying to limit engagements to about fifty a year. Often returning to colleges, universities, wineries, and concert halls on a regular basis—usually at two- or three-year intervals—Brubeck had, until recently, avoided club dates. Then the October 1993 week at the Blue Note in New York turned out to be a pleasure, so Modica signed Dave for a repeat in 1994. European tours, especially to England, continue, but are now spaced two years apart.

Ever since Dave Brubeck became a big business, his legal affairs have been attended to by top-notch attorneys, beginning with James R. Bancroft. Today, Brubeck's attorney and third in this roster of key support compatriots is Richard Jeweler of San Francisco, who was hand-picked right out of law school by Bancroft. The hard dealing for record contracts and other major situations falls to Jeweler, who also runs Dave's publishing company, Derry Music. Derry is an affiliate of Broadcast Music, Inc. (BMI), which licenses all of Dave's compositions, both jazz and formal. Iola says that Richard is one of the inner circle of associates who is "part of the family." Jeweler's value to the Brubecks cannot be overstated; Dave, like most musicians, is no manager of financial affairs. He needs a tough guardian when it comes to making deals and signing contracts.

Dave has chosen to slow the pace, but it is clear that no thought of retiring has ever crossed his mind. Thus, Modica, Gloyd, Jeweler, Moore, and—as ever—Iola are principal players in seeing that Dave's career continues on a smooth course—all bumps and obstacles anticipated and cleared.

CHAPTER TEN

Dave Brubeck has clearly amassed enough close, enduring musical and business relationships to fill more than one lifetime. Many of these compatriots warrant the designation "part of the family."

Time to Expand Horizons

There's Dave Brubeck the pianist, Dave Brubeck the innovator in jazz, and Dave Brubeck the composer. The last category requires further division. Brubeck has a long list of melodies to his credit. Some are sentimental; some are swinging. Some touch the heart. Others tease the intellect. But he, in the same sense as Charles Ives, Leonard Bernstein, or Aaron Copland, is also a contemporary American composer. That's a description he chooses, in reference to his large-scale works. Brubeck has written both secular and liturgical music and lots of it.

The influences on his liturgical music are derived from his family and from the Bible. His mother had a solid, Protestant religious foundation. That, together with his tests of faith when he was seriously injured and later when he had undergone heart surgery and had witnessed the worldwide effects of war, poverty, and inhumanity—all of these have created in him a strong religious conviction. Later in life he became a Roman Catholic. Correcting a widespread and often-quoted error in writings about him, Dave says he is not a convert to Catholicism. "I never had belonged to any church. I was never baptized before. I was the only son in the family who wasn't baptized a Presbyterian. It was just an oversight."

The excitement and ebullience that fill his jazz combo performances have their counterparts in the sheer exultation that fills his liturgical and secular compositions for large groups of singers and orchestral groups.

Religious music is a side of his work that is separate from his usual output; much of it has been misunderstood or misinterpreted by both audiences and critics who do not understand the role that faith plays in Dave's professional as well as his personal life and, therefore, seem puzzled by his use of jazz idioms in liturgical settings. However, the large-scale compositions have been praised and recognized as pioneering ventures.

Often, Dave's own first hearing of the complete work has come at its first public performance. Rehearsals are conducted episodically, broken up by instructions, repetitions, and changes. So, while he has the continuity in his head, the unbroken composition often doesn't reach his ears until it is performed before an audience. Combine that with his improvising during the playing of his scores, and the sense of on-the-spot creativity begins to be appreciated. Most of his music calls for improvisation, which makes some listeners uncomfortable, even though improvisation lies well within the tradition historically established in western music—for example, the cadenzas called for in concertos from the sixteenth century on. But while it is expected and accepted in earlier music, it raises eyebrows among some critics today. Brubeck stresses that the improvisations are optional and that the works can stand on their own without improvisation.

Newspapers often find it difficult to categorize Brubeck works; reviews of his classical music have often appeared under the bylines of pop or jazz reviewers, who equate the name of Dave Brubeck with jazz. While that is not surprising, considering the half-century of jazz that bears his name, it puts jazz critics in situations outside their normal focus, and formal music reviewers assigned to his debut performances have been confounded by his jazz rhythms and use of the Dave Brubeck Quartet as a musical voice of the twentieth century in baroque orchestral settings. This kind of music is complex and, for many people, not easy to understand. Although all of

Dave Brubeck's compositions are taken seriously by the composer, in what follows in this chapter, the large-scale works will be referred to as his "serious" music, for lack of a better term. It has been called "cerebral" and "intellectual," but never dull.

An English choral director, calling him to confer on a performance of one of Dave's choral works, was surprised to hear that the composer is, in fact, a world-renowned jazz musician. He had heard only the oratorios for which Dave has become increasingly respected.

Dave Brubeck, after years of being pigeonholed as a jazz pianist, became acknowledged as a jazz composer; now, he is being compared with some of the major composers of the twentieth century. When he recorded his most recent excerpts from his large-scale compositions, Brubeck called the album *New Wine*. The title comes, he explains, from the New Testament where Peter confronts a crowd in an evangelistic fervor days after the crucifixion: "Peter is saying, 'This crowd of people can't be drunk. It's only the third hour of the day (which I think is nine o'clock in the morning). It's not new wine that they're drinking, it's the voice of the Holy Spirit.'" This "voice" rings out in his choral compositions and his works for large ensembles, musical creations that are jazz-based in some instances but utterly different from the music millions of jazz fans have come to associate with the Dave Brubeck Quartet. For these compositions, Dave works with the Bible, using texts adapted or written by his wife, Iola, a fine lyricist.

Dave is not the first Brubeck to compose serious music. His brother Howard, who wrote many works for symphony orchestra, chamber orchestra, and chorus, created a major score, *Dialogues for Jazz Combo and Orchestra*, in 1956. When the New York Philharmonic's Leonard Bernstein, himself a jazz buff, studied it, he scheduled its performance with the New York Philharmonic and the Dave Brubeck Quartet in a 1959 concert at Carnegie Hall.

The basis for Dave's liturgical music comes from a wide exposure to religious ideas, which he credits to his parents. Bessie Brubeck pursued an interest in Presbyterian, Methodist, Christian Science, and other philosophies, and through her, Dave was exposed to many doctrines. Of his father, Dave says, "I never heard him talk about God once in my life." Dave characterizes Pete Brubeck as having been "naturally religious, very honest, and forthright," with no particular doctrine, accompanying the family to whichever church Dave's mother was attending at the time—mostly Presbyterian and Methodist.

Dave wrote formal music in his twenties—a ballet was completed at age twenty-six. Early on, his talent for composition was evident to jazz writer John Hammond, who reviewed Brubeck's appearance in 1951 at New York City's Birdland jazz club, noting a "complicated and cerebral" quality to the music that set it apart from what Hammond called the "clichés of Dizzy Gillespie and the stereotyped screechings of Stan Kenton." More significantly, Hammond noted a "restless and ambitious" quality in the budding jazz composer, and predicted: ". . . it is quite possible that he might desert the field of jazz playing and devote his time to composition." Dave did not sacrifice one for the other; he did both.

As a composer, Dave prefers to hear his own music without his improvised interludes. However, his major works are often enhanced for the audience in live performances when they can see and hear the composer improvising in the center of the large choral groups and orchestras. It is the same as getting the full realization of a piece by Pierre Boulez or John Cage with the active participation of the composers.

Public awareness of Dave's serious compositions surfaced with a 1968 Biblical oratorio, *The Light in the Wilderness*. Scored originally for organ, percussion, and choir, it was later expanded to a mixed chorus of one hundred voices (augmented for its premiere, during emphatic passages, to five hundred voices), organ, and a full orchestra plus elaborate percussion (including Indian tabla and Middle Eastern instruments). It followed Iola's adaptation of the Biblical text, telling of Christ's forty days in the wilderness, the temptations, the Sermon on the Mount, the selection of the disciples, and the commandment to love one's enemies as one loves one's neighbors.

Even with such an awesome theme and vast vocal and instrumental resources, Brubeck did not abandon the jazz idiom; the score of the seventy-minute work calls for voluntary improvisation—at the opening of one section, the score instructs the orchestra: "Each player makes warlike sounds of his choice."

The meters are typical Brubeck, with a lot of syncopation. The choral parts stretch the limits of the voices, due partly to Dave's admitted lack of knowledge of vocal limits. "I wasn't really aware enough of the ranges, so I looked them up in a book," he says. "They had sopranos from middle C to high C above the staff, and so my first piece had high Cs for all the sopranos. Some choral directors would look at the score and decide it couldn't be done; others got their soprano sections to sing this high C. This is what comes from my being ignorant. Now, of course, I rarely write that for a soloist, but when the entire soprano section hit that high C, it became my favorite choral sound in the entire piece."

Not the stuff of Handel or Bach clearly, and yet the mix of jazz, conventional harmonies, unconventional rhythms, atonality, spirituals, and Middle Eastern themes was received with passionate approval at its premiere in February 1968, with Erich Kunzel leading the Cincinnati Symphony. One critic, who attended the preview performance at the University of North Carolina under the direction of Lara Hoggard, found it so polished a score that he said it could not have been the composer's first choral work. It was compared to Carl Orff's masterful, though hardly religious, *Carmina Burana*, and was called "a minor masterpiece" by *Time* magazine reviewer Alan Rich.

Even Dave was surprised by the wide public acceptance of *The Light in the Wilderness*. In the four years after its premiere in 1968, it was performed more than one hundred times in the United States, Europe, and Australia, was given a televised performance in the National Cathedral at Washington, D.C., and was recorded in 1970 by Decca, to which Brubeck had been loaned out by Columbia Records. It has recently been released as a CD by the Musical Heritage Society, again with Erich Kunzel and the Cincinnati Symphony.

Not all of Dave's non-jazz music is liturgical; he has written secular music experiments and celebrations, all uniquely Brubeck, maintaining his polyrhythmic and polytonal approach. The quartet is often presented playing against—or with—a symphonic ensemble.

Dave's first such work was the 1963 *Elementals,* for jazz combo and orchestra. The title comes from a short story Dave had read while a student, that told of two people deeply in love who were thrown into a prison cell with no food. After they had been starved, a single crust of bread was put in the cell. Which would have more power over their actions, love or hunger?

"The music starts with a heartbeat—*dum,* da-*dum,* da-*dum,* da-*dum,* da-*dum,*" Dave says, "and from the beginning to the end that heartbeat in the same tempo will work no matter what is super-imposed over it. You superimpose 15 over it, where I do in some spots, and it's still going. Or if you superimpose a waltz, or a 4/4 or whatever."

Elementals was his expression of the idea of "the universality of man. The elemental heartbeat is what ties mankind together. It's universal to all people. Therefore, rhythm is the element in music that is universal—not harmony, not melody. And the underlying pulse is the heartbeat. When people say that *music* is the universal language, they haven't had the experience I've had playing the music of different cultures such as India and Africa and Iran and Iraq. *Rhythm* is what it is, and the basis of that is the human heartbeat."

Elementals was written at the invitation of Rayburn Wright, who taught arranging at the Eastman School of Music in Rochester, New York. Wright tells of Dave's hesitancy to take on the assignment of making a full orchestra swing, and of putting it together with a jazz combo, especially one that specialized in improvised music, com-posed on the spot.

In his own liner notes for the Columbia LP disc he conducted, Wright defines the task: "How did it happen that a huge orchestra of vast tonal resources and schooled discipline could collaborate with a small, sensitive jazz quartet and still produce a spontaneous jazz performance? It is certainly true that real jazz moments cannot be planned in detail or written in advance—spontaneity is a real thing and the imitation is easily spotted." But, he continues, jazz and classical artists can complement each other when they are given a broad structure to work in, and then are left free to stretch their artistic limits.

Elementals also broke through the legendary Brubeck depend-ency on others for orchestrations of his musical lines. Dave told Wright: "I can't orchestrate for symphony orchestra, but I'd write a piece for piano, and *he* could orchestrate it. He said 'Great, indicate the orchestration in the piano part: If you hear something for

French horns, just write 'Fr. horns.' So I did the first movement. Wright said, 'This is fine. I can follow you completely. The next one, why don't you work on a full score, and if it's wrong, I promise you I'll change it.' He didn't change anything. He wrote back, 'Continue.' So I wrote the third section. He did say I would be long remembered by French horn players. 'There's one thing here that's probably too hard but let's leave it.'"

On August 1, 1963, the score got its premiere performance at the Eastman School of Music in Rochester. It combined and contrasted the symphony orchestra's charted score with the Dave Brubeck Quartet's improvisations, but even the symphony score called for some spontaneity, allowing conductor Wright to extend or condense sections, while calling for the Quartet to choose those orchestral sections against which it wanted to play. *Elementals* drew a standing ovation.

When Columbia's Teo Macero proposed putting the score on vinyl with a full-scale orchestra of top musicians; Dave, Paul Desmond, Joe Morello, and Eugene Wright gathered under Rayburn Wright's baton, and the seventeen-minute *Elementals* went into musical history. It has since been recorded with Dave, Gerry Mulligan, Jack Six, and Alan Dawson and the Cincinnati Symphony conducted by Erich Kunzel.

Some of Dave's large works follow his early tonal experiments, with more than one theme being played simultaneously. One such is *They All Sang Yankee Doodle,* commissioned by the New Haven Symphony Orchestra for the American Bicentennial celebration in 1976. It starts and ends with the music of American Indians, because, says Dave, "They were here before we got here, and they're probably going to survive what we've ruined." He adds, somewhat fatalistically, "I hope somebody does."

He describes *They All Sang Yankee Doodle* as "an autobiography, made up of memories and snatches of tunes imprinted from my early childhood: hymns and Bach chorales from the church next door where my mother was choir director and the cowboy songs and turn-of-the century ballads that I have always identified with my father."

The score carries a series of national themes—Great Britain's "Hail, Britannia," Russia's "Meadowlands," Germany's "O

Tannenbaum"—each played against a background of the American "Yankee Doodle."

The piece represents some of the mixture of his own social heritage: being raised until age twelve in a small town where the Fourth of July was the biggest event in town, yet living in a community whose streets bore the names of Spanish pioneers, in a house that had belonged to his English grandfather and Polish grandmother, and which was located near the Catholic church where each year a Portuguese band would lead the parade on All Saints' Day. Not surprising, then, the panorama of international influences played against the unifying American patriotic theme that emerged as *They All Sang Yankee Doodle*. Dave dedicated it to Charles Ives, whose *New England Triptych* has a similar form.

New England was the setting for four pieces: *Once When I Was Very Young, Autumn in Our Town, Two Churches,* and *How Does Your Garden Grow?* The last was created in 1988 for *NorthEast Magazine;* Art for All; and The Advest Group, a Hartford, Connecticut, insurance firm and was performed by the Gregg Smith Singers.

Brubeck has written two ballets in addition to that first one from his mid-twenties. *Points on Jazz,* originally written for the American Ballet Theatre as a two-piano piece, was later orchestrated by Howard Brubeck. The original two-piano version was recorded for Columbia by duo-pianists Arthur Gold and Robert Fizdale. It has gone out of print. The other ballet was *Glances,* choreographed by The Murray Lewis Dance Company and orchestrated by Darius Milhaud. Some of these works are in vaults, with searches now in progress to find tracks that were never released. Many of these unreleased tracks were the victims of commercial time limits dictated by the formats then available for releases—LP discs, primarily—and tapes never released that are still waiting to be heard.

While his secular serious music is performed only occasionally, Dave's liturgical scores—only a few of which have been recorded— are performed with regularity, especially at seasonal events: Christmas, Easter, and Martin Luther King's birthday.

It is Dr. King whose text is quoted in *Gates of Justice,* a cantata written in 1969, one year after the civil rights leader was assassinated. The work was proposed, Brubeck recalls, by three rabbis in 1969 after a series of anti-Semitic incidents in New York City. It was commissioned by the University of Cincinnati's Conservatory of Music and the Union of American Hebrew Congregations through the auspices of the Corbett Foundation. Dave said that Rabbi Charles Mintz, who was a member of the Cincinnati Ecumenical Council, heard Brubeck's moving Christian oratorio, *Light in the Wilderness* and asked afterwards, "What about us?"

Brubeck was uncertain about taking on the project; he professed little knowledge of Judaism, although he knew some Hebraic modal music and was aware of Darius Milhaud's *Sacred Service,* premiered in San Francisco when Dave was Milhaud's student at Mills. Rabbi Mintz later recalled, "I told him, 'I'll worry about Judaism; you worry about the music.'" The cantata's premiere was given at the dedication of the Rockdale Temple in Cincinnati.

Elements of the Hebrew scriptures, the *Union Prayer Book* and the works of Hillel were combined by Iola Brubeck along with some of her original writings to create a libretto that urged Black and Jewish citizens to focus on their similar histories of enslavement and suffering; indeed, *Gates of Justice* is a call to envision the brother-hood of all people.

The music contains elements of Hebraic melodies and Black spirituals and blues, with interlacing bridges carrying the thematic matter back and forth from chorus to soloists. The soloists include a cantorial tenor and a Black baritone; the musical styles are mixed with jazz, rock, spirituals, and traditional elements—"just as a congregation is a mixture of individuals," Dave explains. There are celebrations, and warnings of unmet needs. A shofar—the ancient Hebrew ram's horn that was used to sound alarms and to summon worshipers—opens the piece, and Isaiah's call for piety and justice is a central theme, but there is more. "The deeper my involvement in the composition," Dave says, "the more apparent it became that I was no longer thinking in terms of social justice, but to the more basic relationship of man to other men and ultimately to God. A paradoxical truth became shockingly clear: we call upon God in our distress, yet the divine instrument of transforming society is man himself. Man is good."

To illustrate this idea, Dave and Iola combine Hebrew texts, primarily from the prophet Isaiah, and a quotation from Dr. King: "We must live together as brothers, or die together as fools." To emphasize the Old Testament references to "all people" and "all generations," the score blends and overlays verses from the Hebrew sage Hillel and the Psalms with musical messages from The Beatles, folk songs, Simon and Garfunkel, Chopin, and contemporary jazz and rock.

One reviewer described *The Gates of Justice* as "epic" and said it comprised "some of the most melodic writing of Brubeck's career," comparing it to Leonard Bernstein's *Mass* and the devotional portions of George Gershwin's *Porgy and Bess*.

The cantata was recorded by Decca after its October 1969, premiere by the Cincinnati Brass Ensemble, led by Erich Kunzel, with the Westminster Choir and soloists McHenry Boatwright, bass-baritone, and Harold Orback, tenor.

There is a bitter message in the Nixon-era cantata, *Truth Is Fallen,* which takes its title from Isaiah's prophetic warning: "Truth is fallen in the street, and Equity cannot enter. None pleadeth for Justice, none pleadeth for Truth."

Commissioned in 1971 for the inaugural concert in the Midland, Michigan, Center for the Arts, the work was a Brubeck family affair: texts by wife Iola and son Christopher were adapted from Biblical prophecies and combined with Dave Brubeck's music to produce a stirring portrait of pre-Watergate America, then deep in Vietnam atrocities, deceptive home politics, and a generational battleground. A more contemporary text could hardly be found. Matched to the prophetic writings of Isaiah, it called for human redemption by humans, rather than from a divine messiah. The work is scored for soprano, orchestra, and chorus and includes elements of rock and jazz improvisation. The rock ensemble sometimes plays against a percussive martial beat, and the music is complex and polyphonic. It was recorded in 1973 on Atlantic by the Cincinnati Symphony, the St. John's Assembly Chorus, and the New Heavenly Blue rock group.

A choral setting of "Truth," a poem by Robert Penn Warren, was commissioned by the Vietnam Veterans Ensemble Theater and premiered by the Gregg Smith Singers under Russell Gloyd's baton in 1988.

A commission by Our Sunday Visitor, a Catholic publishing company, led to Dave's creating a contemporary mass, which he called *To Hope! A Celebration.*

This commission was also a challenge: no five-hundred-voice choirs, no elaborate orchestral arrangements, the mass had to be performable either in a concert setting with full orchestra or by amateurs, in any setting.

To Hope includes the traditional Kyrie, Sanctus, Amen, Agnus Dei, and Gloria. The score contains only brief portions of the poly-rhythms (notably in the Alleluia) that typify Dave's music, making it more accessible to average musicians. Jazz improvisation is allowed in the score, but is not required. This kind of "simplified Brubeck" draws a mixed reaction from the composer himself: "As a composer, sitting there listening, I prefer it without the improvisation, but as a performer bringing in a new element and reaching more people, I like to see the jazz or improvisational elements."

The mass opens with a line, "Shout joyfully to God, all you on earth," yet another affirmation of Dave's personal optimism and sense of hopefulness for the fate of humanity. He describes the internal joy he had while composing the mass: "Working with a great religious text makes you go into a wonderful kind of euphoria. Every moment of your day, and even sleeping at night, is involved with this text. The rite of the Mass has been around for more than a thousand years; it's probably one of the greatest texts a composer can work with. It does something for you personally while you're working on it; you know you're absorbed in a very good thing." The Public Broadcasting System broadcast a documentary on the process of composing the work.

The mass was called a "virtual cacophony of cultural influences" by one reviewer; others called it simply, "a triumph." It has been performed in cathedrals and concert halls. Most surprising of all perhaps, it was performed at the Montreal International Jazz Festival on July 3, 1987, to a rousing ovation. Dave dedicated the fifty-five-minute performance to his friend, violinist Stephane Grappelli, who was in the audience.

The title *To Hope* comes from Brubeck's basically optimistic philosophy, embodied in an address he gave at Mills College in 1982 while accepting an honorary doctorate. He told the students at his alma mater, "What is really important in the community, in the worst of times, is often music. It's the cement for the community that holds it together, and the thing that gives it hope."

The 1980 mass led to another large-scale composition, the 1985 work, *The Voice of the Holy Spirit: Tongues of Fire*, given its premiere in Cincinnati by the St. Edwards Music Ministry from Richmond, Virginia; the Cincinnati Choral Society; and the National Pastoral Musicians Convention Orchestra, conducted by Russell Gloyd.

Evangelistic and prophetic texts were woven into the sometimes-improvisational score. Again, Dave harked back to his childhood in Concord, California, where he had been taken to a fundamentalist church by his babysitter and had witnessed the congregation speaking in tongues while his mother was rehearsing the choir at the Presbyterian church next door. This experience is recalled in the imagery of the Pentecostal narrative wherein the Disciples receive the power of the Holy Spirit with tongues of fire and a rush of wind, declaring the wonders of God in many languages. To Dave, it was not a chaotic picture, but a universal portrait. The concluding passage, prophesying comfort and light to the people, was selected after he turned to his wife, daughter, and two friends for advice. They unanimously chose the Ephesians 6:13: "Be strong in the Lord and in His mighty power."

The work was not unanimously praised. It won enthusiastic applause at a prepremiere performance, where a reviewer termed it "a powerful and ambitious work." The use of the Quartet in the jazz section was praised for its smoothness in the transfer from orchestra and chorus, and the performance was "nothing short of spectacular." But at its premiere before a convention of pastoral musicians, a critic compared Brubeck's use of oratorio rounds to "Row, row, row your boat," declaiming against "musical culture shock" in the blending of seventeenth-century and twentieth-century thematic matter, and said the Middle Eastern voicings sounded "like a klezmer band going avant-garde." The review went on: "Before the piece was half over, the exits were doing a brisk one-way business." Yet, even that writer scolded the walkouts: "Mixing classic oratorio forms with jazz and Middle Eastern tonalities takes some getting used to. Instead of leaving, the audience members should have stayed and studied Brubeck. Amidst this clash of styles, he was the picture of calm . . . the epitome of a pastoral musician."

"What the reviewer did not care to recognize," says Dave, "is that this was a convention with overlapping meetings, which probably accounts for many of the people who exited during the performance."

Warmer receptions greeted Brubeck's 1975 Christmas choral pageant, *La Fiesta de la Posada,* which retells the story of the birth of Jesus in vivid passages and Latin rhythms. The sound evokes the childlike images of the *piñata,* a papier-mâche container filled with goodies that is broken to shower sweets on those under it, and the awe of the Nativity among a people still impressed by the wonder of miracles.

The tradition of Las Posadas is enacted annually in Mexico and parts of the United States. The Brubeck composition based on this tradition was given a Honolulu premiere by conductor Robert LaMarchina and the Honolulu Symphony, for whom it was written. It was recorded four years later by Columbia Masterworks with the Dale Warland Singers and the St. Paul Chamber Orchestra led by Dennis Russell Davies. Excerpts from *La Fiesta de la Posada* are often performed by the Brubeck Quartet in jazz concerts.

Upon This Rock was commissioned as an anthem for the 1987 visit of Pope John Paul II to San Francisco; Russell Gloyd conducted the score at San Francisco's Candlestick Park.

Brubeck's 1978 oratorio, *Beloved Son,* was premiered by the Bethlehem Lutheran Church Choir, Carillon Choristers, and the American Lutheran Church Women Convention Orchestra, for whom it was commissioned, led by Richard Sieber. The three-section composition contains poetic images from texts by the Lutheran poet, Dr. Herbert Brokering, that tell of the events in the Garden of Gethsemane; a twelve-tone theme establishes the sorrow of Jesus and is sung by a solo baritone over a small chorus of children's and women's voices representing the believers; a militant theme begins the march to Calvary; and a jubilant finale celebrates the triumph on the cross.

Pange Lingua Variations, subtitled *A Celebration for Sacramento,* was created for the California capital city's Cathedral of the Blessed Sacrament, where its premiere audience in 1983 filled the pews, and its performers filled the rest of the edifice: the Sacramento Symphony Chamber Orchestra, the Sacramento Chorale, the Northminster Presbyterian Chapel Bellringers, and the Masterworks Chorus—plus, of course, the Dave Brubeck Quartet, all conducted by Russell Gloyd.

The thirty-five-minute work combined Iola Brubeck's English translation of St. Thomas Aquinas's text with the original Gregorian chants in Latin. It is, as composer Brubeck comments, an attempt to "telescope, in a few minutes, two thousand years of an ancient hymn's history."

His research had shown that the sixth century melody was likely based on a Roman march, which in turn was probably derived from an even older Hebrew chant. On this theme he composed six variations. For later concert performances by the Quartet, one of the variations—the march—has become a showcase for drummer Randy Jones.

The premiere of *Pange Lingua Variations* included Dave at the piano, son Chris on bass, Randy Jones on drums, and Bill Smith on clarinet. The occasion afforded the composer his first opportunity to hear the work played through without interruptions. Brubeck turned to the audience after the performance and told them it was a miracle.

Critics praised it for its "joy, fervor, adoration, and . . . tremendous emotional content." The third of six movements calls for a sudden and unsignaled change from Gregorian chant to improvised jazz, and it invariably jars audiences and critics alike. One called it "marvelous, but mystifying."

The most-often performed of his choral works is *La Fiesta de la Posada*. Other works are *Lenten Triptych: Ash Wednesday, Easter, Bless These Ashes,* premiered in Fairfield County near his Connecticut home in 1988; *In Praise of Mary,* a three-movement work performed a year later by the Brown University Chorus and Grace Church Boys Choir in Cranston, Rhode Island; and *Joy in the Morning,* based on three psalms, commissioned by the Hartford, Connecticut, Symphony and performed by that group and the Hartford Chorale on June 1, 1991.

The latter work is a call for healing. The first version was written before Brubeck underwent an angiogram to identify heart problems that eventually led to heart surgery a decade later—when he wrote the choral version. Taking Psalm 30 ("Weeping may endure for a night, but joy cometh in the morning.") as its base, he adds Psalms 120 and 121 as sources of strength. The music is typically Brubeck: arrhythmic passages amid calm and tranquil phrases.

Dave dedicated it to his cardiologist, Dr. Lawrence Cohen, who was seated next to the composer at the premiere. After a very chaotic, arrhythmic orchestral interlude, the musical pulse became a steady, heartlike beat. Dr. Cohen whispered to his patient, "We are back in sinus [normal] rhythm!"

The Hartford Courant described *Joy in the Morning* at its premiere, celebrating the thirtieth anniversary of the University of Connecticut Health Center, as "a deeply felt piece that defies easy categorization. There are parts that have an old-fashioned, nineteenth-century oratorio sound; there is an earnest fugue; then again, there are lush passages that could have been lifted from the soundtrack of some sweeping cinematic epic."

The audience loved it.

Among his most recent liturgical scores are *When the Lord is Pleased,* based on several proverbs and psalms, and *Hear the Bells Ring,* a song inspired by Christmas.

Now, Dave is turning to other inspirational musical sources as well. His 1992 work, *Earth Is Our Mother,* offered a chance to explore Native American music anew. Listening to tapes of authentic tribal music from the Smithsonian Institution awakened in him hitherto unnoticed rhythmic nuances that tied in with sounds remembered from childhood experiences on the California ranch, where he grew up listening to an Indian cowboy, Al Walloupe, singing Miwok tribal songs.

Doing research into the Native American heritage was stimulating. He found that the United States Constitution may have been partially based on the Iroquois tribe's governing codes, that 60 percent of the world's food is based on Indian produce. "The Indians were the foremost horticulturists that ever lived," he says. "We're only just discovering what we destroyed in destroying these people and these cultures." The title and text are derived from a speech attributed to Chief Seattle, addressing the President of the United States when the Native Americans were being asked to sell their land. The most famous quote is, "How can you sell the sky or the land?"

Scored sparsely, the piece's rhythms are sounded by drummers and echoed by rattles and gourds; the orchestra is a partner to a baritone saxophone solo and mixed chorus. The cadence rises and falls like clouds passing across a sky, the intensity growing and the sense of doom and injustice sounding out against a call for hope and fairness.

The Chief Seattle text is of uncertain authorship, but another portion of the text, authenticated by Iola as coming from the northern tribal chief, predicts "These shores will swarm with the ghosts of my tribe. There is no death, only a change in worlds."

"To think," Dave says, "that all those years ago, this man predicted everything that's happened, knowing what would happen if he had to sell the land to the White people. In the words attributed to Chief Seattle, he pleads with them to respect the land: 'Teach your children to respect the streams, the woods, the rivers, the fish, the animals, because whatever happens to the beasts soon happens to man.' Here's this beautiful speech that we'll probably keep ignoring. We're cutting the redwood trees; he was saying, 'Don't cut the forests and don't kill the salmon.' When we were kids here in California, salmon were so thick all you could see were their backs in the stream when they were coming to spawn. Now there's a fifth left or less, and some species aren't even coming back. He's saying, 'Will you leave the land in the same state that you got it?' Of course, we didn't. And he didn't understand—that's why it opens, 'How can you sell the sky or sell the land? Or how can you sell the sparkle of a river?'"

In a 1993 concert in Seattle, Washington, Dave invited Andy De Los Angeles, chief of the nearby Snoqualmie tribe, to read that portion of the text onstage. Chief Seattle's great-great-great-great-granddaughter attended the performance.

While *Earth Is Our Mother* does not propose to be authentic Native American music, the inspiration is clear.

"The Native American derives great strength from his songs, which are often conceived in a spiritual trance, in visions or in dreams, and handed down as a sacred legacy from one generation to another," Dave says. "My original title for this piece was *The Web*, because I was so struck with the imagery of the web as a metaphor for the tracery of interrelationships amongst all things, live and inanimate. When the web is mentioned in the text, I tried in the music to capture the shimmering consequence of the slightest touch upon a single delicate strand."

Earth Is Our Mother marked yet another beginning for Brubeck.

It started a series of compositions Dave and Iola are leaving as messages to their own children. "If someone else wants to listen to them, fine," he says.

Commissioned by the Marquette Choral Society and performed (to "thunderous applause," one reviewer said) *Earth Is Our Mother* was performed at the University of Northern Michigan in Marquette, a return to the campus setting that seems most comfortable to Brubeck and most enthusiastic about his music, whether jazz or formal.

Writing these works for college performances afforded Dave a chance to work with the students who would be performing them. The interplay between a man who has become a jazz institution and yet another generation of music students has worked out to be mutually rewarding, the students gaining in-person, one-on-one experiences with Dave Brubeck, and Brubeck seeing his work prepared and performed with special care.

Accompanying him to the campuses for these sessions were his wife, Iola, and producer-conductor Russell Gloyd, along with musicians who make up the requisite Quartet. At various times, these have been Randy Jones, Bill Smith, Jack Six, Bobby Militello, or any one of Dave's three sons who currently perform with him in various four-piece combos.

In any of his composing or performing venues, Dave Brubeck has never forgotten that his breakthrough into fame came with the 1953 recording of a live concert at Oberlin College. The mix of formal scholarship, academic excellence, and student enthusiasm pulses through his composing, whether it be short jazz, large-scale serious, or improvisational. It is what has carried him forward from that first awakening at Mills College, working under Darius Milhaud to stretch the musical envelope, to develop new musical metaphors, and to find new modes of expression for his compulsive drive to make people listen.

Time for Reflection

It's not surprising that Dave Brubeck, almost sixty years a performer in 1993, should be sensitive to what the critical world thinks of him as a pianist, a composer, a leader, and an innovator. As he moved into his seventies, still playing to capacity audiences all over the world, continuing to make new, well-selling recordings and still composing, he began to question and counter critical notice that tended to dismiss his importance as a pianist.

There were friendly exchanges with author Ted Gioia, himself a pianist, founder of Stanford's jazz studies program and author of *West Coast Jazz* (Oxford University Press), a 1992 overview of modern jazz in ferment in California between roughly 1945 and 1960. Gioia devoted several chapters to the Brubeck story: well researched, well written, and as complete a study of a fascinating period of change as you're ever likely to encounter. Gioia says, "Although Brubeck's influence on other players (especially through his experimentation with odd meters) is quite evident, it is rarely acknowledged, at least in jazz circles." He goes on to note, "Although the jazz world may be sparing in its praise, the music community at large accepted Brubeck as an innovator long ago, as does the listening public."

Dave began to send Gioia copies of old clippings that attested to his influence on other players such as Keith Jarrett, Keith Emerson, Cecil Taylor, and Denny Zeitlan.

Says Dave, speaking of Gioia, "Perhaps we differ on definition of 'influence.' I certainly don't have a school like Tristano, or an exclusive bop style like Bud Powell. However, music teachers worldwide have used my piano books to illustrate my various approaches to jazz, such as counterpoint, polyrhythms, polytonality."

Beginning about 1955, Dave's brother Howard was transcribing Dave's solos as they had been improvised on recordings. These were published in a series of "piano albums" after the release of almost every new Columbia album. There was also a collection called *Dave Brubeck Simply Revisited,* made up of simplified arrangements of Brubeck compositions, aimed at young pianists. Keith Jarrett often has commented on how valuable these pieces were to him, growing up in musically-deprived Allentown, Pennsylvania.

Dave continued, "Paul [Desmond] used to say that we as a quartet touched upon many areas in our exploration for new ideas and new sounds that were later taken up and developed exclusively and as a style by other groups. I think this is true. I also think that many young pianists who heard me felt that some of my music was accessible, and learning from it, they could analyze and develop their own styles. This is the way my great teacher, Darius Milhaud, approached his students; from his classroom have come electronic composers, twelve-tone serialists, romantic modern composers, jazz arrangers: music of all styles based on his solid musical foundation, but not a mirror image of Darius Milhaud.

"Certain pieces of mine are so difficult that they remain largely unplayed by other pianists, but are still influential. 'Tritonis,' *Elementals,* 'Time In,' 'The World's Fair' are a few examples of what I mean. This is not easy music to improvise on, and it's only recently that a piece like 'The Duke' is beginning to be explored as a 'playing' tune. It was performed as a song before, but pianists are now beginning to stretch out on the changes. I have had to grow into some of these pieces myself.

"I have heard about my lack of impact on the jazz world so many times that I'm afraid it has by now become gospel. But the facts dispute the so-called 'common' knowledge." Dave notes, in conclusion, "I've found out that once something is in print it is quoted over and over again."

It's not the purpose of this book to dig deep into old clippings and rehash comments that were made in print as Brubeck and the Quartet emerged as popular icons. The reviews were extremely varied. Some called his playing "loud," "harsh," "unswinging." At the same time, as prickly a critic as John Hammond could be, he wrote, "Brubeck is a trail-blazer in music, uncompromising in his standards. Although his music is complicated and extremely cerebral, it has tremendous drive and surprising warmth. Despite an amazing variety of rhythmic patterns, his music always swings and occasionally rises to heights of unbelievable excitement." That was in 1951.

In 1993, the dean of jazz critics, Leonard Feather, said, "I don't think Dave was an influential pianist. He is certainly an individual pianist. He has a style very much his own, but I don't think it's influenced many people. People nowadays tend to be inspired by McCoy Tyner and other people who have come up since Dave. I think Dave is an extremely talented pianist, but I don't think his influence on others has been that strong. But, without question, he is a major figure in the jazz world."

Pianist Marian McPartland, hostess of National Public Radio's *Piano Jazz* weekly program, after repeated invitations, persuaded Dave to appear on her show; the resulting hour session is available on a Jazz Alliance CD. She has this assessment of Brubeck's talents: "Not everybody considers Dave a terrific jazz pianist, but I've always felt that he was not *only* a wonderful composer but an extremely inventive player."

Marian remembers, "Joe Morello used to tell me that one thing about Dave was that he never got into a rut and always started every tune in a different way than he had before. That's Dave's big thing—never get stale. I love to play with Dave. I find him a very compatible piano partner. We once played together at a concert at Avery Fisher Hall in New York. I thought it was wonderful. The highlight of the night was not just when he played with me, but when he played by himself.

"I think Dave's a one-of-a-kind musician in the way he keeps writing and composing, all against the terrible odds of his health. He just, somehow, has a will to go on and be better and better!"

McPartland has often performed and recorded Dave's compositions. There's no better tribute from one musician to another.

In 1993, critic-author-composer-editor Gene Lees had these comments: "First of all, I think of Dave as a composer who plays piano, rather than a pianist who composes. I think Dave thinks of himself that way. Dave's sometimes a very uneven piano player. He told me once, 'Those polyrhythmic factors don't always come off,' and he's right. When they do come off, it's very exciting. When Dave brings it off, my God, he'll blow you away! Dave does something jazz musicians ought to do: Dave takes chances. It doesn't always work, but when it does it's marvelous."

Lees also made this point. "Dave is one of the most gorgeous ballad players I know. And I happen to know that a lot of players, like Oscar Peterson, think very highly of Dave. I've had private conversations with him on this subject. And don't forget, Dave Brubeck was Paul Desmond's favorite piano player. Dave could 'comp' for Paul absolutely exquisitely. It worked. It's one of those rapports in jazz like Louis Armstrong and Fatha' Hines, Joe Venuti and Eddie Lang: they just had a rapport that was quite remarkable. And, in the Quartet, they had the serenity and solidity of Gene Wright and Joe Morello, so Dave and Paul could be all over the place."

Looking at the larger picture, Lees says, "When I was in my twenties, say in the 1950s, Dave Brubeck—I won't say just Dave Brubeck, the Dave Brubeck Quartet—virtually defined jazz. They just cut a swath across the whole thing. Who else was on the cover of *Time?* Dave opened up the college market for jazz. I would have to say that Dave looms as one the major figures."

Thus, Feather and Lees agree on the phrase, "one of the major figures." That begs the issue of his lasting importance as a pianist. Perhaps, in the long run, it will have to be left to the individual, non-professional listener to whom Brubeck has provided challenges and, as an enduring popularity and record sales attest, pleasure. Try to get last-minute tickets to a Brubeck concert.

It's therefore interesting that, when Dave recorded his first solo piano album in forty years and Telarc released it in late 1994, critical acclaim was universal. Some critics, mellowed by time (and perhaps by Dave's choice of material—mostly variations on standards), appeared astounded at the poetry, symmetry, and sheer joy of playing that this "somewhat underrated" pianist evinced through twelve selections ranging from "It's the Talk of the Town" to "Just You, Just Me," the title tune. There is a nearly eight-minute series of variations on "Brother, Can You Spare a Dime?" very frugal in concept, but polytonality is of no import in this collection. What strikes both educated and casual listeners is the tenderness, the looking back with wonder that marks most of these one-take performances. That's especially true of Dave's own "Lullaby," "Briar Bush," and "Strange Meadowlark." This last title, recorded on several previous occasions, is powerfully swung here, and the absence of a rhythm section is not missed at all.

Brubeck is sensitive to loyalty, or the lack of it. It's an essential element in his own personality, and he has, on occasion, been deeply hurt by disloyalty in others. It was a real blow then when, in 1971, Columbia Records showed Dave the door. For seventeen years, the Brubeck Quartet had been the hottest seller in Columbia's jazz catalog. During most of that period the label had intelligent, musical, visionary executives in Goddard Lieberson and Irving Townsend and such producers as George Avakian and Teo Macero. Then a new president, Clive Davis, arrived, bringing with him the rock superstars and an overriding interest in the current pop scene and the large immediate sales it could bring. Artistic merit was not an immediate priority it seemed.

Dave learned, six months after it happened, that Columbia had not renewed his contract. This occurred with no negotiation and no notice to either Dave or his agent. "I don't think they even told my producer, Teo Macero," says Dave. "I was let go, I think, mainly because Columbia wanted me to use the Fender electric piano and their electric bass; they owned a piece of the Fender Company. They called in Miles Davis, and they called in me. I refused to do it. Miles did it. Maybe Miles had to do it because, or so I am told, he was way overdrawn on his royalties. How crazy the world works. People thought how advanced was Miles' thinking when he used these Fender electronic instruments, but maybe it was the money. Maybe he had to do it. He wasn't exactly happy, but it turned out great for him, whereas they didn't want me on the label unless I used a Fender

Rhodes. It's funny, at that time I believed in the acoustic piano and the acoustic bass, but later on I changed my mind about the electric bass because of the way my son Chris played it. And Darius played Fender Rhodes piano—ironic!"

A side-bar to this is that shortly after the "firing" took place, Dave got a call from Goddard Lieberson, apparently recruited to talk to Dave as an old friend. Lieberson said that the sales department, about to have a world-wide CBS convention, wanted Dave to make a "star" appearance. Lieberson had been moved upstairs to be head of CBS, then the parent company. Puzzled, Dave nonetheless agreed to show up. "I ran into Tony Bennett [another Columbia star] and I said, 'I feel strange. I'm no longer with the company.' Tony said, 'Neither am I!'" Columbia was letting go almost all of its established quality stars (by then referred to in the trade as "middle-of-the-roaders," or "MOR") in favor of rock and only rock.

The final twist is that Bennett returned to the label in 1986 to do an album a year and, in 1992, hit it big in sales and won a Grammy for *Perfectly Frank,* and 1994 saw Tony become a major star with a whole new generation because of appearances on MTV. And Brubeck became only the third artist, after Bennett and Billie Holiday, treated to a box-set, multi-CD retrospective release. The label is now owned by Sony (the Japanese, especially those in the executive suite, are far more interested in jazz and big bands than Americans); it has reissued many Brubeck Quartet albums in the digital CD form, including previously unissued tracks. Dave has again become a major Columbia money-maker, although obviously not making new recordings for his old label.

After Columbia, he went to Atlantic and then to Carl Jefferson's Concord Jazz, for which he recorded (most often with the Quartet consisting of Dave, either Jerry Bergonzi or Bill Smith, Chris Brubeck, and Randy Jones) some of his best work. Dave left Concord only because MusicMasters promised an opportunity to record, and release some of Dave's large-scale works for voices and orchestra, an expensive series of projects. It's often been said that the quality of the recording at Concord, especially of the piano itself, has never been equalled, although Dave now says that he likes the piano sound on the new Telarc recordings even better.

Reflection for Dave and Iola Brubeck was always a luxury, so busy were they with things current. When, as Dave moved into his seventies, they were prodded into thinking back by the Columbia retrospective, increasing numbers of interviews (including the many done for this book), and the luxury of some leisure time for themselves, there were many highlights to recall. Iola had the advantage of having, for many years, written the semi-annual "Dave Brubeck Quartet Newsletter." Done for fans all over the world, it has always been full of news about new records, concert schedules, and the doings of each member of the family. In the Winter/Spring, 1992–93 edition, for example, her observations about European audiences are both affectionate and insightful:

> Since 1958 the DBQ has toured England and the Continent almost every year, sometimes twice a year. Observing the audiences this autumn reminded me of those earlier years when the crowds were young and the atmosphere electric. Some of these same people, now greying and past middle age, are still in the audience. They bring their souvenir programs, concert tickets, and LPs that date back 30 or more years, to be autographed anew. They bring their children and grandchildren to share the experience of a live concert.
>
> For the most part, the audiences that greet the Quartet in Europe these days, especially in Austria and Germany, are surprisingly young. One sees students and young professionals, not yet born when the DBQ first appeared in Europe. I imagine they perceive the Dave Brubeck Quartet as a venerable institution, it having been a part of the established culture since the time they were born. In their enthusiastic response, it is apparent that the Dave Brubeck Quartet is not just a link to the past, but for them an example of continuing jazz history.

Iola had this comment: "One reason, I think, for the longevity of the music created by the Quartet has been Dave's continual desire to push at the boundaries of the small group format, experimenting with larger forms integrated with jazz, thereby risking loss of that part of his following who knew only the popular 'Take Five,' but gaining the respect of serious listeners of each new generation. The musical vision of all the various new Brubeck groups has been taken up in recent years by growing numbers of younger jazz musicians, the neo-traditionalists, who recognize that in order to move forward, they must know more about where jazz has been and how it evolved into its present form."

The Quartet has been repeatedly honored by being asked to play at White House functions, going back to the time when John F. Kennedy invited the group to be part of an outdoor concert on the Ellipse. Then the Lyndon B. Johnson administration had the DBQ entertain at a state dinner honoring King Hussein of Jordan. In the early spring of 1988, Dave and a new incarnation of the Quartet played for Ronald and Nancy Reagan at the White House for a party which was a part of that year's Governors Conference. One governor in particular was deeply impressed with what he heard: Bill Clinton made a point of coming over to Dave after the concert to discuss jazz and Brubeck's approach to it in particular.

For Dave, the most significant and, undoubtedly, the most satisfying White House appearance occurred in 1994, when he renewed his acquaintance with now-President Clinton. This was a year in which Brubeck enjoyed a whole catalog of new honors. These included election to the *Down Beat* Hall of Fame (long overdue), being named San Francisco Jazz Festival Laureate, and an honorary doctorate from the University of Duisburg in Germany. But the crowning tribute came at the White House, where President Clinton presented Dave Brubeck with the National Medal of the Arts. The President told the honoree, "You know, I learned to play sax listening to Paul Desmond on your 'Take Five,' and, Mr. Brubeck, I can still almost do it!"

Remembers Dave, "Jazz Galleries International had arranged for President Clinton to be given the number one serigraph of my own original manuscript of my 'Blue Rondo a la Turk.' He told me he was absolutely thrilled to receive it and that he could sing the entire piece from memory, 'including the hard parts.' He then proceeded to do so." And, says Iola, "I'll never forget Bill Clinton, with a schoolboy's grin, singing 'Blue Rondo' as he walked with a happy, buoyant step beside Dave. 'Two events have made my day. This morning I saw Aristide leave for Haiti and now I've received the manuscript to "Blue Rondo."'"

The 1988 Reagan White House invitation had an extraordinary and unexpected consequence—the appearance of the Dave Brubeck Quartet at the Moscow Summit. On hand that evening in 1988 was Russell Gloyd, Dave's conductor, producer, and all-around manager. Gloyd had grown up in Washington, had served as a member of the music staff in the White House when he was in the army, and knew protocol well enough to be sure that the Reagans would have to entertain the Gorbachevs in Moscow during the coming summit get-together. So Russell broached the subject to Nancy Reagan. "I knew that I wanted to be there," remembers Gloyd. "I told her that I would like very much to show her the Russian reaction to the same pieces we had just played there in the White House. She seemed very excited about that, so I made a dub of the Arts and Entertainment network broadcast of the Quartet's last night in Moscow, made during our trip to the Soviet Union in March of 1987."

It was a busy time for the Brubecks, who set out on a European tour. While the Quartet was in Paris, the Reagan-Gorbachev summit was announced. Two days after Dave and Iola returned home, the White House called to ask if the Quartet would be able to go to Moscow with the White House party. "That called, without hesitation, for an unqualified yes," remembers Gloyd. "But we had a problem. We had engagements booked in that period of time. I had to call places like Ohio State University, saying, 'We will not be able to perform, but we can't tell you why. However, when you finally hear the reason, you will understand. And believe me, you'll hear about it.'" All venues accepted the cancellations, having found from previous experience that almost nothing could cause the ultra-dependable Brubeck to miss a scheduled appearance.

The White House insisted that the Quartet's participation be kept a secret until the entire package was announced by them. When it finally was, it made the news all over the world. Ohio State called Russell Gloyd back to say, "We do understand. In fact we feel as though we're participating in the summit by making it possible for you to be there."

Gloyd says, "You have to put this in perspective. There was Perestroika, the whole awakening of the Soviet Union, the whole concept of what was taking place at that time in world history. This was the first time there was hope of a real chance for an understanding between the East and the West. For Dave to be the representative artist meant everything to everyone who was close to us."

Nothing is easy when you're dealing with the White House and, sure enough, it took what Gloyd calls "major, major negotiations" to work out all the details of travel, accommodations, who could go, and what they would play when they arrived. One concession was that they were allowed to take Eugene Wright along as a special guest, meaning, with Chris Brubeck, two bass players. It was quickly clear that the White House staff looked upon the Quartet as an unnecessary annoyance; in Moscow, Gloyd had to repeatedly invoke the magic words, "Mrs. Reagan," as in "Well, it's funny, but when Mrs. Reagan and I discussed this, there was no problem." End of discussion. No one wanted to cross that line.

The big day came, and it was very hot in Moscow. The humidity was stifling. According to Gloyd, "The ballroom at Spasso House [the United States embassy] was shielded on all sides by curtains, not so much for the protection of Reagan, but for the protection of Gorbachev because there were lots of assassination plots on him. You couldn't have a more hot or stuffy affair. Reagan was struggling to stay awake. He was just totally exhausted from this trip. I walked in thinking that this was the hardest room Dave had ever had to work in his life. They had Soviet and American people mixed at all the tables, but you could just see and feel that nobody was talking to anybody.

"They made the obligatory speeches and Dave was introduced. Then, it was like out of a Hollywood *B* movie. All of a sudden, everyone just came alive. Dave started in and the first tune he played was 'Take the "A" Train.' It brought down the house. People were up and cheering. I'll never forget Bob Dole—he looked like a little kid. He had his one good hand raised above his head like he was at a football game. He'd turn around, and there was a Soviet general, loaded with medals, doing the same thing! They looked at each other like, 'You like Brubeck? I like Brubeck! *We* like Brubeck!' It went like that for twenty minutes. Dave played the greatest single twenty minute set in his life.

"Right after the performance was over, Dave and I were rushed over to the hotel where all the international television people had set up shop. You know how jaded international press people are, especially the television people, and all the top people were there. When Dave walked through, all these hardened old-hands came out and applauded as he headed for CNN. Bernard Shaw did the interview. They played a little tape from the press pool, and Shaw asked Dave a few questions about his reaction to the situation. Dave said it was the most incredible moment in his life. At the end, Shaw turned to Dave and said, 'I have to tell you, on the part of everyone here that watched you, there was not a dry eye among us when you started playing '"A" Train.' We realized we couldn't have had any greater ambassador from the United States than you.'"

The next day, at the Bolshoi, George Schultz, the secretary of state, was coming through the reception line, Gloyd says. "He sees Dave, he breaks his own security guard, comes over, and hugs Dave and says, 'Dave, you helped make the summit. And today everyone on both sides was talking about it. They found common ground. You broke the ice.'"

Another passenger on the plane to Moscow with Dave and his group was an important negotiator in nuclear matters. Gloyd remembers him as a grim-faced official whose job had been to try to determine just how much nuclear armament was necessary to blow up Russian cities. "For years," explained Gloyd, "he had been looking at Soviet cities simply as targets, not people. His current assignment was to talk with his Russian counterpart. The day after the concert, the talks took a new turn. The American official told me, 'We decided, after today's meeting, that instead of going our usual separate ways that we'd take a walk. We walked along the Moscow River, and he showed me pictures of his grandkids, and I showed him pictures of my grandkids, and we looked at each other remembering that we'd devoted our lives to killing each other. We parted with a different look at the whole picture.'"

Dave, Chris, Randy Jones, Bill Smith, and Eugene Wright were introduced to Gorbachev, who turned out to be more of a jazz fan than anyone suspected. In fact, when Dave started playing "Take Five," according to Gloyd, "Gorbachev's translator, the guy with the bald head and the beard, was poking Gorbachev and saying, we could figure out, 'See, I told you they'd play it!' And Gorbachev was mimicking the drum solo with both hands."

The entire Brubeck entourage headed for home, giddy with excitement, but ready for some quiet moments. By then, home for Dave and his family had long been Wilton, Connecticut.

To own a home—a permanent place to put down roots—had always been a dream for Dave and Iola Brubeck. The war, studies at Mills, and the subsequent hard-scrabble effort to eke out a living in the real world stymied any hope of realizing that dream. None-theless, shortly after the war, they had taken a one-thousand-dollar war bond Dave's father had given them and purchased a piece of what was considered unbuildable property at 6630 Heartwood Drive in the Oakland, California, hills.

Iola remembers, "We used to take the train from Stockton right through that area when we were in college, and we fell in love with the spectacular view of San Francisco Bay." One reason the view was so terrific was the extreme drop-off on the fifty- by one hundred-foot lot; only a little of it was level. San Francisco, unlike Los Angeles, hadn't been a place where innovative design and construction had encouraged homes to be built in such precipitous circumstances.

About that time, through a mutual friend, the Brubecks met Dave "Bev" Thorne, a young architect still studying at UC Berkeley. It was a fortuitous meeting and one that eventually established Thorne as a designer of unusual and difficult-to-build houses, many of them for celebrities. Looking at the Heartwood property, he quickly said, "cantilever." Soon he began drawings, still not aware of who this young piano player was or of his potential. Thorne was uninvolved in music of any kind, let alone contemporary jazz.

The Brubeck Trio was at that time working in central Oakland's Burma Lounge, and one of Thorne's roommates finally tipped him off. "We're all going to be famous someday, Bev, not because of what we've done as architects but because you're working with Dave Brubeck. He's headed for the big, big time." It was years, however, before Thorne realized that not all musicians were the straight-arrow, sober, family-oriented fellows that he met in Dave.

While design of the Oakland house started in 1948, years went by before money could be raised to start construction. The house was to be L-shaped and to include a music room, a master bedroom, and two bedrooms for the (then) two kids, Darius and Michael. Thorne and the Brubecks would meet at the Burma Lounge and later, at the Blackhawk in San Francisco, after Dave finished the last set, gener-ally about two in the morning. It was decided to retain an enormous rock on the property and build the music room around it. Eventually, Thorne embedded a large piece of glass in the side of the rock to form a table on which Dave would compose.

Thorne recalls that, "Every so often, Olie would call and say,

'We need another bedroom.' That was as Chris, Catherine, and then Daniel arrived. The two children's bedrooms became four tiny cubicles as a result."

With Dave's career finally on the rise and a Columbia Records contract in the bank, and some money accumulated, builder Arthur Hovanitz started construction in 1953, working at it all winter. It was finished in 1954, with the Brubecks moving in only to temporarily move out, while Dave fulfilled a summer-long series of contracts in Los Angeles. While they were gone, Thorne lived in the Oakland house, marrying while he was there and enjoying his honeymoon in a home that eventually became featured in *House Beautiful*–type magazines and industry journals all over the world.

The house was also the scene of a live broadcast on *The Ed Sullivan Show* in 1960, and the music room served as a recording studio for a number of piano solo albums (sessions done just before dawn to accommodate Dave's working hours and to avoid noise from passing aircraft).

Just when the family's financial picture was becoming brighter, disaster struck in the form of a lawsuit. As recounted in chapter six, Dave had made a television film, *Stompin' for Mili*. Apparently the finished project was never commercially released, but prior to that, Dave had obligated himself to two former students from the College of the Pacific who were trying to get started in the television business. Dave, to help them, agreed to work on a "spec" basis to produce at least a "demo" for a show to star Dave. Then, one of them got involved in a brouhaha in a Hollywood nightclub, and Dave decided he surely didn't want to do business with such a character, overlooking the fact that he had signed an exclusive contract with the guy.

When *Stompin' for Mili* was shot, amid considerable publicity, the two sued Dave, Columbia Records, and the coproducer on the show, Dave's record producer at the time, George Avakian. The Brubecks' attorney made it clear that, because Dave's signature was on a contract, there was no way he could win before a judge, and the case was settled out of court.

Dave and Iola say, "They took almost everything we had, except the house, which we had luckily homesteaded under California law. They got the money we had set aside all year for income taxes, because that was in a bank. They attached that account and every asset they could get their hands on."

"The only good thing that came out of this," says Dave, "was that I hired James R. Bancroft to handle the lawsuit, and he told me never, ever to sign a contract without his say-so. To this day, that's the way it is."

Another pivotal role played by Jim Bancroft came in 1959 when Dave decided he'd had it with the road. Record royalties were becoming substantial. He announced he'd just stay in San Francisco, having become established enough to find enough work to pay the bills. But the family, still shaken by the lawsuit, simply had no money put aside to send the kids through college. Bancroft, remembers Dave, said, "It's going to be a lot tougher for your kids than for you. My advice is, don't quit. Your best years are just coming. Move the family east. There's plenty of work there nearby."

About this time, Irving Townsend, a major figure at Columbia Records, was transferred west to become head of production for the West Coast. He arranged with the landlady for the Brubecks to take over his house in Wilton, Connecticut, at eighteen hundred dollars a year. Most of Townsend's neighbors were musicians and other artists. It was serene, with spacious fields and a barn, and within a few hours of New York City, Boston, and many other places where the Brubeck Quartet was in great demand.

The dramatic move, encouraged by Bancroft, was done on a one-year test basis. It meant an equally dramatic change for the other members of the Quartet, especially Paul Desmond, but it worked out wonderfully well for all concerned.

Dave and Iola found a piece of land across town they thought they could love as much as the Oakland hillside where they had acquired all the available surrounding property. Again Bev Thorne was called to duty. In 1961, he began designing what became known as the "Wilton Hilton." The original Oakland house was built for a grand total of $27,500 and had twenty-two hundred square feet of living space. Now Iola, as concert fees and record royalties finally began to justify the move from California, decided to go all-out and make the Wilton place perfect for the family and as a music studio for Dave.

It started with a five-acre parcel on Millstone Road, but Dave, finding property values extremely low compared to those they'd known out west, kept buying adjacent parcels until he had acquired twenty-five acres of rolling, wooded land, complete with an always-running stream. This was eventually dammed, creating a substantial backyard pond. The first design for the house had twelve thousand square feet, but again the prudence of the Bancroft law firm counseled caution, and this was cut back to seven thousand square feet of eminently congenial living space. Included were nine bedrooms—none too many as the years went by and grandkids multiplied.

The rock motif of the Oakland home was followed through in Wilton with a section of a rocky ledge found on the site extending into the new house along one side of a majestic stairway that curved down to the living room and, down another level, to the music room and sometime recording studio.

Hanging there is a self-portrait by Darius Milhaud. This came about, Iola says, when the Oakland house was first built and Milhaud, Dave's mentor, asked for one square foot he could call his own. Milhaud had lost all his possessions in escaping Europe on the eve of World War II. He asked the Brubecks for a piece of ordinary typewriter paper, on which he sketched a self-portrait. It was organized around themes from his best-known work, *La Creation du Monde*. Iola had the paper original converted to a copper etching. It occupied the place of honor on the hearth in Oakland and has an honored spot in Wilton.

On a small island in the pond behind the house, reachable by an arched bridge, Dave had built a small gazebo with a deck. There is where he came to do most of his composing, standing up to spare his back, using an easel with a keyboard mounted above. In the pond, fish jump and geese squawk to their young. Such tranquillity didn't come easily and certainly would never have been achieved but for the stability and determination of one person, Iola. As oldest son Darius has always insisted, Iola was the anchor.

Dave and Iola celebrated the fiftieth anniversary of their marriage with nearly two hundred family members, associates, and friends at the historic Claremont Hotel in Oakland in September of 1992.

Darius Brubeck was not the first to speak, but his was the first toast of the evening, and he set the tone for all that followed. Like most of his siblings, Darius talks easily and eloquently as would be expected from someone as well and broadly educated and as cosmopolitan as he. To begin, he offered this explanation of his generation of Brubecks. "I'm merely a normal person," he said, "who had Lenny Bruce as a baby sitter."

Then he said, "Music has been a tremendous source of recreation, solidarity, and relaxation and ambition and competition and disappointment and success for my generation of the family. But the real binding force has been the home, and the home has been always and forever the domain of Iola. The combination of the artistic and the domestic has been well met and well married, and unlike most of the rest of us younger folks, Dave and Iola got it right the first time." The toast was made and the cake was cut.

Earlier, Iola and Dave had taken turns introducing everyone in the ballroom at the historic old hotel. Once a glamour spot in the West, from which virtually every major big band in the nation broadcast coast to coast, the Claremont has been well maintained and still retains much of its glory and prestige. It has ties to the Brubecks, as well.

Said Dave, "We chose the Claremont Hotel for many reasons. One of them was that on my mother's side, her father—my grandfather—drove the stagecoach right over the hill behind us on Fish Ranch Road from Concord to Oakland, every day. They stopped at the Fish Ranch Restaurant, which was on the other side, right where the [Caldecott] tunnel starts that you go through now. They had a meal and then continued on to Concord. Grandfather on my father's side owned seventeen hundred acres of Oakland hillside right where we're now standing. He was a guy who could not stand people very much. He always kept moving. When people moved in, he moved out. If he'd stayed here you'd be talking to the owners of this place!"

As Iola has pointed out, these, their dearest friends, had come from all over the country and many different fields. Not all knew one other, so that introductions were in order. Some guests asked to come forward and reminisce, and their remarks were both poignant and entertaining.

Dave began the introductions this way, "If you knew my father, you knew he was a great cowboy. He was a great roper. Some of you remember him from the old days. I think of this room as being one of his lariat ropes that kinda ties every table together, and if you could get a loop this big, he'd rope you all in. Some of you are sitting next to old cowboys, who are sitting next to musicians. In our family, that's a tradition. But to us, you're all joined in this great love and great importance to our life."

Among the musicians introduced were members of the original Octet, Bob and Dick Collins, Jack Weeks, Bill Smith, and Ron Crotty. Dave Van Kriedt (who died in late 1994) had just returned to Australia. There were seven Trio and Quartet bass players: Ron Crotty, Wyatt "Bull" Ruther, Jack Weeks, Eugene Wright, Norman Bates, Jack Six, and Chris Brubeck. There were four Quartet drummers: Joe Dodge, Lloyd Davis, Dan Brubeck, and Randy Jones. Joe Morello, hampered more severely than ever by his virtual blindness, hadn't been able to make the trip from his home in New Jersey.

On hand also were Frances Lynn, who had in 1946 sung with The Three D's at the Geary Cellar; Newell Johnson, lead trumpet with "The Band That Jumps" that Dave had taken to Globin's in Lake Tahoe just before World War II; and Gerry Mulligan, who, later in the evening, would guide a marathon jam session until the wee hours of the morning.

There were all the members of the immediate family, their spouses, and children. Members of the "working" family, including Juliet Gerlin, George Moore, Nancy Peterson, who handles book-keeping, and the legal eagles of the Bancroft office were all introduced. Russell Gloyd, of course, was omnipresent and was the overall master of ceremonies.

On hand were old friends such as Harold Meeske, who had introduced Dave and Iola, and Bob Skinner, the kid-next-door in Concord, whom Dave first saw when Bob was just a half-hour old. Wonderful memories warmed the room.

Army buddies such as Ernie Farmer and Jerry Jones were introduced, as was Cal Tjader's widow, Pat. So was Ramona Burris (Dutschke), the Indian lady who had been Dave's mother's piano-teaching assistant. Taking a bow (and later playing) was bassist Vernon Alley, whom Dave and Iola had gone to hear on their very first date—at a jazz club in San Francisco.

There too was Basil Johns, Dave's "biggest fan" who was actually the very first to record Dave (solo, on some primitive acetate recording equipment). Architect Dave Thorne and his wife, Pat, were on hand to recall the conception and realization of the Brubecks' first real home. Peter Levinson, the publicity specialist whose work had so helped promote countless Brubeck recordings and personal appearances, took a bow. And there were many more, including countless in-laws, aunts, uncles, nieces, nephews, and cousins, each introduced with affection by Iola or Dave.

The wine (supplied by Jim and Jane Bancroft from their own vineyards) flowed, and the food filled the tables, and there was a quality of intimacy that belied the size of the party.

Missed was Dave's oldest brother, Henry, who had died some years before. But brother Howard was there. Said Dave, "Howard and his wife, June, started going together in Concord in high school—or maybe it was grammar school. Those of you who know me well know how badly I needed Howard. He wrote down all of my recordings. He'd just take them off the records and transcribe them 'cause I was too stupid to do any of those things. He wrote the piece that we recorded with Leonard Bernstein and did many innovative things and has been my teacher and my right-hand man."

Howard was to survive only another four months, dying suddenly after surgery. The loss was a terrible blow for Dave and came in mid-February 1993, when Dave himself was at a low ebb. Exhaustion had set in after a European tour undertaken when he was suffering from an unshakable flu bug that had, in fact, first hit him at the time of the anniversary party. This, in turn, led to heart arrhythmia problems that put Dave in the hospital in Glasgow and London. "That was a nightmare, the whole tour," Dave said upon arriving in Florida for a final concert before taking a mandatory rest. Sick, weak, worried, Dave had nonetheless fulfilled obligations with the same tenacity that had been a hallmark since his earliest performing days.

According to Iola, "He only missed one concert. That was in Glasgow. One other, in Austria, had to be rescheduled to the end of the tour. It's been a long fight back, and the doctors may have overdosed him with medications to keep him going, but they're backing off now, and that's a big help." Contrary to some reports, Brubeck did not suffer a heart attack. Some years before, he had undergone multiple-bypass open-heart surgery, which had been a complete success.

By May of 1993, Dave was on the road once more, a little weak in voice and movement (excepting his hands) but gaining strength. By mid-June he had begun to sound like his old self, and the concert schedule, both with symphony orchestras and the Quartet, resumed at a steady pace. In Saratoga, California, on a steaming hot night, August 1, trusted sidekicks Jack Six on bass and Randy Jones on drums flanked Dave on the outdoor stage at the historic Montalvo Mansion on the hillside, and Bill Smith played, as had Paul Desmond, in the nook of the Baldwin grand. Smith had brought along his electronic bag of tricks which permitted doubling of his clarinet, with echoes and other effects that at times made him sound like an entire reed section.

With Iola and Russell Gloyd making sure all physical arrangements were secure and coping with relatives, reporters, promoters, and fans backstage, Dave moved slowly to the piano. His stoop (the result of that long-ago diving accident in Hawaii) was perhaps more pronounced, his step more deliberate, his frame yet thinner, and his voice, during the very few moments he devoted to talk, less than robust, but then he played, and the never-diminished vigor and delight obviously inspired his fellow musicians.

It was about 105 degrees still at nine o'clock at night; the audience, several thousand strong and perched everywhere but in the treetops, used their programs as fans and consumed unlimited quantities of bottled water and soft drinks—and some wine and a few martinis. Dave had a big jug of water handy, and it was a relief to see him partake of it generously.

He began easily, quietly, but in no way tentatively, playing his "The Duke," which took the ensemble into an Ellington medley. The old magic remained, and for the rest of the evening, he could do no wrong. The audience (gray hair side-by-side with rosy-cheeked children and grandchildren) cheered and applauded every solo and every piece, however obscure the time signature might have been.

After intermission, the youngest Brubeck son, cellist Matthew, joined the Quartet. Matthew is even taller than Dave. He is six feet, eight inches, as thin as his Dad, but with a new, trim beard that makes him look older than his years. First came the traditional opener, "St. Louis Blues," and the cello, plucked or bowed, swung as mightily as the piano, clarinet, bass, or drums. Matthew was seated front and center on what appeared to be a small soap-box (so as to be low enough for his cello) and cued by Dave, he delivered chorus after chorus that was pure inspiration, perhaps more than even his father's inventions. Dave was enormously proud and pleased, and some of the most fiery moments of the evening took place during W. C. Handy's indestructible tango-cum-blues.

"Take Five" was, as it almost always is, the finale. It brought the crowd to its feet with recognition, about two bars in. The encore was another audience-rouser, "Take the 'A' Train." Dave left 'em standing up and cheering.

People ask why he should want to undertake a grueling coast-to-coast tour with a different hotel or motel each night, make-do eating, and back-wrenching airplane seats—especially when you know that Dave isn't hungry for money as in the early days, and fame is an objective that was achieved long ago. It can only be assumed that he needs to constantly make music, and performance is that need's realization.

In the later summer of 1993, Dave Brubeck talked of the future. "I would say that plans to do new things are as high now as they've ever been, and we're working on some surprising things that it's too early to talk about. But they will be some breakthrough things, I think."

Brubeck is always concerned about barriers, including, and especially, racial ones. Recalling his Southern tours with bassist Eugene Wright and the refusal of the Georgia college to allow the Quartet onstage unless the single Black in the group was replaced, Dave points out that the final OK came from the governor of the state who assured the college president that the school would not lose its funding if Wright was permitted to perform with his White colleagues. "It's money that often controls the moral policies of everything, including the government," Dave says. "The power behind politics and religion and almost everything, if you get deep enough into it, war or anything, it's going to be greed, money, and fear. Leave people alone, and they'll usually accept goodness.

"What I did everywhere was, if they wouldn't integrate the hall, I wouldn't play. Many of the halls wouldn't allow Blacks to come in, so I wouldn't go onstage. Of course that challenging the system can

CHAPTER TWELVE

work two ways. Sometimes they think, 'Well, if I don't allow Blacks in, I'll lose some money.'

"It was a tough decision, and, meanwhile, it wasn't easy for us. We had police cars in front of the college the whole concert. About that time, Louis Armstrong had a bomb thrown while working down South. It missed the backstage, but that's what they were aiming at."

Certainly the future of music in America depends on tolerance and exposure to a wide variety of things musical. Dave points out that "The Europeans have an advantage because the radio stations there play much more jazz than they do in America. But in this country, it's gotta be mostly hard metal or rap.

"There's no reason for stopping kids in their formative years from getting an all-around education, which we just don't do anymore. Most schools today don't really teach music anymore. When you cut out art, you're losing in culture; you're losing in government; you're losing in industry. Many educators think art isn't important. I could give them an argument it is the most important. When you cut out art, you're cutting the legs off your culture. Yet it's the first to go, and the last to go is going to be the sports program."

The Brubeck story is not high drama. It will never make the supermarket checkout-stand tabloids or a sensational summer novel. There were few periods of great depression or conflict. "I'm lucky that way," says Dave. "The other day I was explaining to my young grandson, Benjamin, that when his dad is out of town playing, that's not a bad thing because he's building for your future. And he's building for his own future. It's how you end up at the end of your life that's very important. I told Benjamin that I'd been able to offer all my kids a college education, and I hated to be on the road, just as your dad [Chris] hates to be gone, but it's good that he's able to go out now so that you can go to school later. I'll bet you if you add up the number of hours a guy who doesn't have to travel to work spends with his kids and compare that with the hours I've spent with my kids, I'll be way ahead. And it's continuing. They still play with me."

Sitting on his tiny, private island in his pond, surrounded by greenery, the singing birds, and the honking geese, and asked whether there was, looking back, anything he regretted doing or wished that he had done, he said, "You know, last night I was reading the Bible in the middle of the night. When I wake up and can't sleep, I grab for that book. And the reading tells me that God fashions each of us for His own reason. I thought, boy, I wish He had fashioned me in a different way in a lot of areas! But then I started really thinking about it. What if I'd been a different kind of musician? Would I have done what I did? The answer is, God probably knew what He was doing. All of us have flaws. Some people are born that they're not going to run fast. They're crippled all their lives. Yet they can achieve so much. I knew one person who couldn't even move anything but his mouth. Using his mouth he managed to create the first computer that the airlines used. Maybe God knew that, if this extraordinary person had everything and wasn't confined to a wheelchair, unable to move, he wouldn't have just sat there using his brain and creating great things. You gotta accept the way you are. I wouldn't change anything."

> The sensitive man sits,
> reading the Bible,
> exploring the origins of life.
> Life with its magical beauty,
> and brilliance.
> Life without boundaries,
> without limitations.
> My Father is sensitive,
> I can see him now,
> reading, lost in a world,
> somewhere on the printed page.
> He is the essence of talent,
> but he has time to care,
> and love me.
> —*Poem by Michael Brubeck*

Discography

Listed here alphabetically by label are Brubeck recordings that were available in the spring of 1995. Only American-issued albums are listed, but European releases, especially reissues, of Dave's extremely abundant recorded performances are even more numerous. Not included are any bootleg or unauthorized recordings. There are many of these, mostly taken from live concerts or broadcasts. The artists derive no royalties, and the quality is generally poor. These, therefore, were not deemed worthy for inclusion, even though they may have some value to the curious and insatiable collector.

Indicated are both CDs and cassettes, as well as LPs where available. Columbia, in particular, retains a storeroom full of unreleased material and can be expected to continue new releases from old recordings as well as reissues.

Every effort has been made to be accurate and inclusive, with sources including the most-current Schwann-Spectrum catalog and Iola Brubeck's quarterly newsletter listings, as well as information supplied by the recording companies themselves. Inevitably, with the constant changes in stewardship and ownership and technology, these lists are subject to change month by month. The collector should use this discography as a starting point. For a very detailed history of Brubeck's recordings (at least through 1990), see the authoritative *Dave Brubeck Discography* by Dr. Klaus-Gotthard Fischer, published by the University of Duisberg, Germany in 1992. Its 232 pages of recording dates, releases, reissues, personnel, labels, recording sites, and cross-references of both out-of-print and current recorded material is invaluable.

A & M

Duets
Dave Brubeck, Paul Desmond
A & M 75021-3290, 1975 (CD & Cas.)

ATLANTIC

Last Set at Newport
Brubeck, Gerry Mulligan, Jack Six, Alan Dawson
From the Newport Jazz Festival, 1971. Atlantic 1607-2 (CD), CS-1607 (Cas.).

We're All Together Again for the First Time
Brubeck, Paul Desmond, Gerry Mulligan, Alan Dawson, Jack Six
Concerts in Rotterdam and Berlin, 1972. Atlantic 1641-2 (CD), SD 1641 (Cas.).

All the Things We Are
Brubeck, Jack Six, Alan Dawson, Anthony Braxton,
Lee Konitz, Roy Haynes
Studio session, New York City, 1974. Atlantic 1684-2 (CD), SD 1684 (Cas.).

Dave Brubeck: Two Generations of Brubeck: "Brother, the Great Spirit Made Us All"
Dave, Darius, Chris, and Danny Brubeck: Perry Robinson:
Jerry Bergonzi: Dave Powell: Peter Ruth (on some tracks)
Studio session, New York City, 1974. Atlantic SD 1660 (Cas. only).

COLUMBIA/SONY

Dave Brubeck: Time Signatures: A Career Retrospective
This four-CD, fifty-one-selection box set is far and away the most definitive Brubeck collection. It includes tracks from Fantasy, Atlantic, Concord Jazz, and MusicMasters masters, as well as many of the best from Columbia, including some vault titles previously unissued. Covers 1946 through 1991. Extensively and excellently annotated by Doug Ramsey and Juul Anthonissen. Columbia C4K52945 (CD only).

Dave Brubeck: Jazz Collection

A two-CD collection taken from the four-CD retrospective *Time Signatures*. Includes performers Paul Desmond, Norman Bates, Joe Dodge, Joe Morello, Eugene Wright, Jimmy Rushing, Carmen McRae, Billy Kyle, Louis Armstrong, Charles Mingus, and Gerry Mulligan. Columbia C2K64160 (CD only).

Jazz Goes to College

Brubeck, Paul Desmond, Bob Bates, Joe Dodge

From tapes of concerts at the University of Cincinnati, University of Michigan, and Oberlin College, 1954. Columbia Jazz Masterpieces CK-45149 (CD), CJT-45149 (Cas.).

Dave Brubeck: Interchanges '54

Brubeck, Paul Desmond, Bob Bates, Joe Dodge

Collection of tracks from two early 1954/55 Columbia albums, *Brubeck Time* and *Jazz: Red, Hot and Cool*. Columbia Legacy CK-47032 (CD), CT-47032 (Cas.).

Time Out

Brubeck, Paul Desmond, Eugene Wright, Joe Morello

Includes classic 1959/60 original tracks of "Take Five" and "Blue Rondo a la Turk." Columbia Jazz Masterpieces CK-40585 (CD), CJT-40585 (Cas.).

Gone with the Wind

Brubeck, Paul Desmond, Eugene Wright, Joe Morello

An especially lyrical, swinging collection of such Southern standards as "Swanee River," "Camptown Races," "Georgia on My Mind," and "Basin Street Blues." Recorded at the American Legion Hall in Los Angeles, 1959. Columbia Jazz Masterpieces CK-40627 (CD), CJT-40627 (Cas.).

Jazz Impressions of Eurasia

Brubeck, Paul Desmond, Joe Benjamin, Joe Morello

Recorded in Columbia's Thirtieth Street studios in New York City upon the return of the Quartet from a long tour (eighty concerts in fourteen countries) of Northern Europe, behind the Iron Curtain into Poland, the Middle East, India, and Afghanistan, 1958. Columbia Legacy CK-48531 (CD), CJT-48531 (Cas.).

Jazz Impressions of New York

Brubeck, Paul Desmond, Eugene Wright, Joe Morello

This album is a result of Dave's taking an assignment to write music for the television series *Mr. Broadway* with Craig Stevens. The idea was to catch the essence of New York City. Recorded in June, July, and August 1964 in New York City. Columbia Jazz Masterpieces CK-46189 (CD), CT-46189 (Cas.).

The Great Concerts

Brubeck, Paul Desmond, Eugene Wright, Joe Morello

Concert performances in Amsterdam, Copenhagen, and Carnegie Hall, New York City in 1958 and 1963. Includes extraordinary performances by Desmond and Brubeck on "Tangerine" and an exhilarating, fast-paced "Take Five." Columbia Jazz Masterpieces CK-44215 (CD), JGT-44215 (Cas.).

Anything Goes: The Music of Cole Porter

Brubeck, Paul Desmond, Eugene Wright, Joe Morello

New York City studio recordings, 1963. Columbia PCT-09402 (Cas. only).

The Dave Brubeck Quartet Plays Music from West Side Story *and Other Shows and Films*

Brubeck, Paul Desmond, Eugene Wright, Joe Morello

The music of Leonard Bernstein, Cole Porter, and Richard Rogers from studio sessions in New York City, 1960, 1962, and 1965. Columbia Masterpieces CK-40455 (CD), CJT-40455 (Cas.).

The Essence of Dave Brubeck

Brubeck, Paul Desmond, Eugene Wright, Joe Morello

Economy-priced collection from other albums. Columbia Legacy CK-47931 (CD), CT-47931 (Cas.).

Time Further Out

Brubeck, Paul Desmond, Eugene Wright, Joe Morello

Extended adventures in polytonality in original compositions. Columbia PCT-08490 (Cas. only).

Dave Brubeck's Greatest Hits

Brubeck, Paul Desmond, Eugene Wright, Joe Morello

Columbia PCT-00289 (Cas. only).

Dave Digs Disney

Brubeck, Paul Desmond, Norman Bates, Joe Morello

All from Disney films. Includes tracks previously unissued. Recorded in Los Angeles, 1957. Columbia CK-48820 (CD only).

The Real Ambassadors

Brubeck; Eugene Wright; Joe Morello; Louis Armstrong;
Carmen McRae; Lambert, Hendricks, and Ross

Designed for Broadway but performed only once—at the Monterey Jazz Festival—the all-Brubeck score with words by Iola Brubeck was built around Armstrong. This 1994 reissue contains material previously unissued in the United States. Columbia CK-57663 (CD only).

La Fiesta de la Posada

This much-performed Christmas Cantata was recorded in 1979 but has long been out-of-print—but now remastered to digital. Brubeck, Dennis Russell Davies conducting the St. Paul Chamber Orchestra, the Dale Warland Singers, and Edith Norberg's Carillon Choristers. Columbia Masterworks 36662 (CD only).

CONCORD JAZZ

Concord on a Summer Night

Dave and Chris Brubeck, Bill Smith, Randy Jones

Dave returned to the rolling grazing land where his father once raised cows, now the Concord (California) Jazz Pavilion, to perform before a capacity audience a group of Brubeck originals, plus a new version of "Take Five," 1982. Concord Jazz CCD-4198 (CD), CJ-198-C (Cas.).

The Dave Brubeck Quartet: For Iola

Dave and Chris Brubeck, Bill Smith, Randy Jones

Recorded live at the Concord Pavilion, 1984. Dedicated to Dave's wife of more than fifty years, Iola, whose name is Native American and whom Dave calls "the strongest inspiration of my life." Concord Jazz CCD-259 (CD), CJ-259-C (Cas.).

The Dave Brubeck Quartet: Reflections

Dave and Chris Brubeck, Bill Smith, Randy Jones

A studio session in Connecticut, recorded near the Brubeck home, December 1985. Produced by Dave's old friend Carl Jefferson (owner of Concord Jazz) and especially notable for the mystic beauty of "Blue Lake Tahoe" and for the trombone playing of Chris Brubeck on "My One Bad Habit." Concord Jazz CCD-4299 (CD), CJ-299-C (Cas.).

The 1987 Dave Brubeck Quartet: Blue Rondo

Dave and Chris Brubeck, Bill Smith, Randy Jones

A collection of Dave's originals, including a tribute to his then-newest grandchild, Elana Joy Yaghsizian, and a new treatment of the classic "Blue Rondo a la Turk." Concord Jazz CCD-4317 (CD), CJC-317 (Cas.).

Paper Moon

Dave and Chris Brubeck, Jerry Bergonzi, Randy Jones

Standards all, including "Symphony," "I Hear a Rhapsody," and "It's Only a Paper Moon." Recorded 1981 in San Francisco. Concord Jazz CD-4178 (CD), CJ-178-C (Cas.). Note: Concord, as of 1995, stopped cassette releases.

·Tritonis

Dave and Chris Brubeck, Jerry Bergonzi, Randy Jones

The title piece is what Dave calls "an example of the place I hoped to arrive at when I began playing." Very polyrhythmic and polytonal. Concord Jazz CJ-129-C (Cas. only). Limited availability as of 1995.

Back Home

Dave and Chris Brubeck, Jerry Bergonzi, Butch Miles

Mostly standards in a 1979 session taped live at the Concord Jazz Pavilion. Concord Jazz CCD-4130 (CD only).

FANTASY

Jazz at Oberlin

Brubeck, Paul Desmond, Ron Crotty, Lloyd Davis

March 1953 concert in Finney Chapel, Oberlin College, Ohio. Considered among the finest recorded performances by the early Quartet. "The Way You Look Tonight," "Stardust," other standards. Fantasy OJC-046 (LP), OJCCD-046 (CD), OJC-5046 (Cas.).

The Dave Brubeck Octet

Brubeck, Paul Desmond, Cal Tjader, David Van Kriedt,
Dick Collins, Bill Smith, Jack Weeks, Bob Collins

July 1950 studio session in San Francisco. Rare examples of the celebrated Octet. Fantasy OJCCD-101 (CD), OJC-101 (Cas.).

Dave Brubeck/Paul Desmond/Dave Van Kriedt: Reunion with Norm Bates and Joe Morello

Quintet studio session of early 1957 in San Francisco. All originals. Fantasy OJC-150 (LP), OJCCD-150 (CD), OJC-5150 (Cas.).

Brubeck a la Mode: Featuring Bill Smith with Joe Morello, Eugene Wright

Three-quarters of the Classic Quartet, minus Paul Desmond, but with Bill Smith on clarinet. All originals. New York City, 1960. Fantasy OJC-200 (LP), OJCCD-200 (CD). Not available on cassette.

Dave Brubeck Plays and Plays and Plays

Dave's original solo piano album. Includes "Sweet Cleo Brown," "Indian Summer," "Two Sleepy People." Recorded in the Brubeck's Oakland, California, home, 1957. Fantasy OJCCD-716 (CD only).

The Dave Brubeck Trio: 24 Classic Original Recordings
Brubeck, Cal Tjader, Ron Crotty

Recorded in San Francisco in 1950. All standards. Fantasy 24726 (LP), FCD-2476 (CD), 5F-24726 (Cas.).

Dave Brubeck/Paul Desmond with Wyatt "Bull" Ruther, Lloyd Davis, Herb Barman

San Francisco studio recordings, 1951/52. Some tracks from concert at Storyville in Boston. Fantasy FCD-24727 (CD), 5F-24727 (Cas.).

The Dave Brubeck Quartet, Featuring Paul Desmond

Some tracks from an appearance at Birdland, New York City, with Brubeck, Desmond, Ruther, and Barman—some with Fred Dutton on bassoon. This collection mixes studio and club recordings. Subtitle is "Stardust." Fantasy F-24728 (LP), FCD-24726 (CD), 5F-24728 (Cas.).

The Dave Brubeck Quartet, Featuring Paul Desmond, in Concert
Brubeck, Paul Desmond, Lloyd Davis, Joe Dodge

Some from Storyville, some from a concert at the Wilshire-Ebell Auditorium in Los Angeles, some studio sessions. Mostly recorded in 1953. Fantasy FCD-60-013 (CD only).

Jazz at College of the Pacific
Brubeck, Paul Desmond, Ron Crotty, Joe Dodge

Dave's third concert at his old alma mater, December 14, 1953. All standards. Fantasy OJC-047 (LP), PJCCD-047 (CD), OJC-5046 (Cas.).

JAZZ ALLIANCE

Marian McParland's Piano Jazz with Guest Dave Brubeck

Edited from a National Public Radio broadcast, hosted by piano legend Marian McPartland. Dave discusses his life and his music and plays both solos and duets with his hostess, including "The Duke," "St. Louis Blues," and "Take Five." The Jazz Alliance TJA-12001. (CD only).

MCA/DECCA

Brubeck/Mulligan/Cincinnati

Brubeck; Gerry Mulligan; Cincinnati Symphony Orchestra,
Erich Kunzel, Conductor

The two soloists are backed by Jack Six, bass; Alan Dawson, drums; and the orchestra. A program of Dave's originals, including "The Duke" and *Elementals.* MCA Classics MCAD-42347 (CD), MCAC-42347 (Cas.).

MUSICAL HERITAGE SOCIETY

The Light in the Wilderness: An Oratorio for Today

Dave Brubeck, Piano; the Cincinnati Symphony Orchestra,
Erich Kunzel, Conductor; with the Miami University A Cappella
Singers and William Justus, Baritone

Originally recorded for Decca on March 19, 1963, this reissue of the most-performed of all Brubeck's large-scale works is available by direct order from Musical Heritage, 1710 Highway 35, Ocean, NJ 07712.

MUSICMASTERS

The Dave Brubeck Quartet: New Wine:
with the Montreal International Jazz Festival Orchestra,
Russell Gloyd, Conductor

Taken from the sound track of a CBC-televised concert of July 3, 1987, during the Festival International de Jazz Montreal in Canada. Orchestral arrangements are by Darius Brubeck, Russell Gloyd, and Dave Brubeck. Bill Smith is the clarinetist with Chris Brubeck, electric bass, and Randy Jones, drums. Includes "Summer Music," "Blue Rondo a la Turk," and "Take the 'A' Train." MusicMasters 5051-2-C (CD), 5051-4-C (Cas.).

Quiet as the Moon

Evolved from a television assignment for Dave to compose background music for the cartoon series, *This Is America, Charlie Brown*. The particular episode for which Dave composed dealt with the NASA space station. Subsequently, sections from the score were recorded in 1988, 1989, and 1991 for release that year. Dave Brubeck is joined by sons Chris, electric bass and trombone; Matthew, cello; and Dan, drums, as well as by Bobby Militello, sax; Jack Six, bass; and Randy Jones, drums. MusicMasters 01612-65067 (CD), 01612-65067-4 (Cas.).

Trio Brubeck

Dave, Chris, and Dan Brubeck, recording at a studio in upstate New York. This family affair is buoyed by their obvious pleasure in playing together and ranges from standards such as "I Cried for You" to originals such as Dave's "King for a Day" from *The Real Ambassadors* and "Bossa Nova USA," played in 5/4 time. "Over the Rainbow" is perhaps the most memorable track, with Dave playing in two keys at the same time, and Chris on trombone expanding on that polytonal concept until soulful swinging takes over. MusicMasters 01612-65102-2 (CD), 01612-65102-4 (Cas.).

TELARC

Late Night Brubeck

Recorded live in early October 1993, at the Blue Note in New York City. With Bobby Militello, sax and flute; Jack Six, bass; and Randy Jones, drums. Included is a long tribute to Duke Ellington, some other standards, and several new songs by Dave. This recording was made during a triumphant stand at the Blue Note, and the performances are so audience-driven that they overcome problems of balance and Dave's illness at the time. Telarc CD-83345 (CD only).

Just You, Just Me

Dave Brubeck recorded this solo piano album, his first in almost forty years. It was done, as Dave said, "in the same way I play at home, one idea calling up another." There are seven standards, and five by Dave. All but one selection was done in a single take. All show Dave with great power in terms of both keyboard technique and inventive concepts, but the melodies are approached with respect and affection. Especially notable, according to critics who had high respect for the entire collection, were Dave's variations on "Brother, Can You Spare a Dime?" "A Tribute to Stephen Foster," and Dave's own "Strange Meadowlark," which ranges from the plaintive to the joyously swinging. Telarc CD-83363 (CD only).

Night Shift

More from the Blue Note appearance in October 1993, this time with Bill Smith and Chris Brubeck joining Dave, Bobby Militello, Jack Six, and Randy Jones. The program is largely standards, among which are "I Can't Give You Anything but Love, Baby," "Yesterdays," and "River, Stay Away from My Door." Telarc CD-83351 (CD only).

The Big Band Hit Parade

An all-star event with Erich Kunzel and the Cincinnati Pops Big Band Orchestra. Ray Brown, bass; Dave Brubeck, piano; Cab Calloway, vocals; Eddie Daniels, clarinet; Buddy Morrow, trombone; Gerry Mulligan, baritone sax; Doc Severinsen, trumpet; and Ed Shaughnessy, drums. Brubeck is featured on "Take the 'A' Train" and "When the Saints Go Marchin' In." In this last, he creates a stunning oasis of introspection and gentle swinging between the torrid choruses by Morrow and Mulligan and the ride-out with Calloway and all soloists a la Dixieland. Telarc CD-80177 (CD), CS-30177 (Cas.).

Dave Brubeck: Young Lions and Old Tigers

Recorded in 1994 and 1995, each selection (excepting one solo track) features a guest playing with Dave. The "Young Lions" include Roy Hargrove, trumpet; Michael Brecker, tenor sax; Christian McBride, bass; Joe Lovano, tenor sax; Joshua Redmond, tenor sax; and Ronnie Buttacavili, flugelhorn. The "Old Tigers" are Dave; Jon Hendricks, vocal; George Shearing, piano; James Moody, tenor sax; and Gerry Mulligan, baritone sax. Regulars Jack Six, bass; Chris Brubeck, bass; and Randy Jones, drums accompany on various tracks. Includes eight new compositions by Brubeck. CD-83349 (CD only).

Mass: To Hope!

A live concert performance in the National Cathedral in Washington, D.C., with 180 voices in the combined choirs of the Cathedral Choral Society and The Duke Ellington School Show Choir. Also with 32 musicians from the National Symphony Orchestra; soprano, tenor, and baritone soloists; and the Brubeck Quartet. Set for release in the late summer of 1997.

Index

Index of Works Mentioned